THE WINES OF
CENTRAL AND SOUTH-EASTERN EUROPE

The Wines of Central and South-Eastern Europe

R. E. H. GUNYON

DUCKWORTH

First published in 1971 by
Gerald Duckworth & Co. Ltd
3 Henrietta Street, WC2

© 1971 R. E. H. Gunyon

All rights reserved. No part of this publication may be reproduced, stored in a retrieval system, or transmitted, in any form or by any means, electronic, mechanical, photocopying, recording or otherwise, without the prior permission of the Copyright owner.

ISBN 0 7156 0592 5

Printed in Great Britain by
Bristol Typesetting Co. Ltd
Barton Manor - St. Philips
Bristol

CONTENTS

Preface		7
1	Introduction	9
2	The lands and the peoples	12
3	The vines and the wines	19
4	Austria	34
5	Yugoslavia	47
6	Hungary	64
7	Hungary: Tokaj-Hegyalja	84
8	Czechoslovakia	94
9	Romania	97
10	Bulgaria	106
11	Albania	112
12	USSR	113
13	Greece	115
Appendixes	1 Soils	119
	2 The Ottoman Turks and their drinking habits	122
	3 The Lenz Moser high-culture system of growing vines	123
	4 Spirits	124
	5 Chromatography	124
	Index	127

PREFACE

A book like this cannot be written without help from many sources and I have shamelessly importuned friends and acquaintances. They have given me unstintedly of their time and expertise and I cannot hope adequately to express the depth of my gratitude. Much of any merit that this book may have is due to them.

In particular, I must thank Pamela Vandyke Price and John Higgins for their invaluable professional criticisms of my typescript; John Gilmour of the University Botanic Gardens at Cambridge who has kept me right on matters of botany and, indeed, of style; Mrs Anna Roche for her great help with German translations; Bernhard Teltscher for lending me the admirable Ampelographical Atlas and for supplying the illustrations of the Slovenian 'winery'; Jeremy Roberts and George Mortimer for giving me the run of their extensive and peculiar wine libraries; Nigel Blundell, Ernst Gorge and Frank Hajak for their special help with Romania, Austria and Czechoslovakia; Douglas Lloyd of the Department of Chemistry at St Andrews; Mr I. Torporczy of the Hungarian Embassy and the staff of Monimpex, Budapest for information about Hungary and photographs; Edward Roche and my colleagues at Edouard Robinson Ltd; those who have been mentioned and acknowledged in the text; others, in many countries, with whom I have corresponded, often delightfully, but whom it is most unlikely that I shall ever meet; and many others, too numerous to name individually, but to whom I am most grateful; and finally my family, without whose tolerance and forbearance my task would not have been possible.

Sandwich. May 1971.

I
INTRODUCTION

This book is being written because when I undertook (having some commercial interest in Hungarian wines) to teach students entered for the Wine & Spirit Education Trust's Diploma courses about the wines of central and south-eastern Europe, I found that there was not much that I could recommend that they should read, and most of what there was to be scrappy, some of it inaccurate and out of date.

I therefore set about collecting information directly from the producing countries. This was not as easy as I had expected; some countries were lavish with help while others appeared to regard my enquiries as attempts to pry into state secrets. And some of the countries, being modern Socialist Republics, were reluctant or even perhaps unable to tell me much about wine-making in their countries under earlier regimes.

At this stage I became interested in the historical background and it was increasingly apparent to me that there is a need for a full study of the viticultural history of this complex part of Europe. It is clear, too, that a true picture of the area cannot be seen by treating each country in its present form as a separate entity. This little book does not claim to be more than a preliminary sketch for the fuller and deeper treatise that must some time be produced, if only because it is plain that much more wine from this part of Europe will be widely exported in the years ahead, and it is natural and right that more and more people, consumers as well as shippers and merchants concerned in its importation and distribution, will want to know all about it; and it is an interesting and absorbing subject.

It was very apparent, too, when I started my classes, that the students, although most of them were fairly senior in the wine trade, came with detailed knowledge of the French and German table wines and of Port and Sherry; rather less but nevertheless adequate knowledge of Italian, South African and Australian wines; but knowing little or nothing about the wines that are the subject of this book – those of Austria, Czechoslovakia, Hungary, Yugoslavia, Romania, Bulgaria and the USSR. These countries contain in areas such as the Burgenland in Austria, the Maribor district and other parts of Slovenia in Yugoslavia, and the whole of the west and north of Hungary what has been described as 'a great European heartland of wine-growing'.

There is also a prejudice, which has grown up since the war and persists in certain parts of the British wine trade itself and among consumers generally, that any wine not made in France or Germany is only fit to be classified under the ugly and indelicate label of 'plonk'. What nonsense! This attitude is not always discouraged by the French and Germans. I am sure that with the sweeping away of ignorance the best of these wines will come to be accepted again as part of the fine ancient tradition of European wine-making, the first and greatest in the world.

It is necessary to record in detail the characteristics, and place- and grape-names for each of the countries covered by this book, but these facts are preceded by some general geographical and historical considerations, and notes about wine-making and the grape varieties common and peculiar to the various countries.

Where an interesting side-track has shown itself in the course of my writing, I have not hesitated to explore it, and I hope this will be of some interest. I have been careful to avoid confusing facts with opinions and hope this is always clear. Where opinions are expressed they are entirely my own and I take all responsibility for them.

There is finally a short note about the wines of Greece. Greece is in many ways outside the culture and traditions which unify most of the other countries covered by this study; but it must be added because Greece is included with the central and south-eastern European countries in the Diploma examination syllabus, and the information may be found useful to those travelling to Greece or eating in the many Greek and Cypriot restaurants.

INTRODUCTION

In referring to distances, areas, quantities, weights and alcoholic strengths I have kept throughout to the decimal measures in general use throughout Europe: linear measurements in metres and kilometres (⅝ mile); areas in square kilometres (0.386 square mile) and hectares (2½ acres); quantities in litres (35.2 British fluid ounces, 33.8 US ounces) and hectolitres (22 British gallons, 26.4 US gallons); weights in tons (a metric ton is nearly equivalent to a British ton); and strength in degrees Gay-Lussac which is the percentage of alcohol by volume (40° Gay-Lussac equals 30° under proof Sikes and 80° US proof).

Some of the countries making the wines discussed in this book are unfamiliar to the general reader and, I have found, not well represented in atlases. The map (printed on the end papers) obviously cannot give all the great detail that would be desirable. All the more welcome, therefore, will be a *World Atlas of Wine and Spirits* edited by Hugh Johnson and to be published this year (1971) by Mitchell Beazley Ltd London. As Mr Johnson has had access to practically the same information as has been available to me, I am sure that his atlas will be found to be a most useful companion to this volume, and of course valuable far beyond this context as it covers the whole world.

2
THE LANDS AND THE PEOPLES

THIS is a study chiefly of the wine made in Austria, Hungary, Romania, Yugoslavia and Bulgaria, countries which all export their wines to Great Britain in increasing quantities: 60,000 hectolitres in 1970 which is about 8 million bottles and this quantity is growing rapidly; briefly of Czechoslovakia, where good wine is made but not yet imported into Britain in significant quantities, and of the USSR which makes wine in the southern Ukraine and particularly in Crimea, a little of which is imported, although Soviet Russia is on balance a large importer of wine from her central and south-eastern European neighbours, together with a postscript on Greek wines. As Greece is in so many ways outside the general area we are considering, I shall not include references to it in this general survey.

These countries, then, lie between latitudes 40° and 50° north, and Vienna is on about the same latitude as Orleans, Prague, a little north of Mainz and Rheims, Budapest in line with Tours and Angers, the significant vineyard areas of western Hungary, Slovenia and southern Austria lie within the latitudes that cover Burgundy; Belgrade and Bucharest on roughly the same latitude as Bordeaux; and the southern boundary of Bulgaria as Tarragona. Their total land area, including Czechoslovakia but not Russia, exceeds that of the whole of France, Western Germany and the Low Countries. The distance from Prague to the Bul-

THE LANDS AND THE PEOPLES 13

garian frontier with Greece is about 1300 kilometres and it is roughly the same from Istria on the Adriatic to the Danube delta on the Black Sea: and that is the same distance as the crow (and probably most international airlines) flies between London and Vienna.

Physically there is a great plain covering most of Hungary, eastern Austria and Slovenia, the Roman Pannonia, and the strip of Transylvania on Romania's western frontier; surrounded by mountain ranges – the high Alps and Carpathians to the north and west, the Transylvanian Alps to the east, and to the west and south the great ranges running from the Alps right through Yugoslavia, Albania and Bulgaria and ending at Mount Parnassus itself to the south. The whole area is unified by the river Danube and its tributaries of which Drava, Sava and Tisza are the most interesting to us.

Austria and Hungary are now entirely land-locked and, of course, Czechoslovakia always has been, but Yugoslavia's long western coastline is tempered by the Adriatic Sea as are the eastern coastal plains of Romania and Bulgaria by the Black Sea. The large lakes of Balaton in Hungary and the shallow Neusiedler lake in Austria are big enough to influence the microclimates of the vineyards that grow round them. The Hungarians claim Balaton to be the largest inland water area in Europe, although I would have thought that the Alpine lakes of Geneva and Constance ran it very close indeed.

The influence of the surrounding mountains and the tempering sea protects the central European countries from the extremes of the Polish and western Russian climate system with its subarctic winters, and gives them short, sharp winters, long, warm summers with late autumns and fairly predictable rainfalls and temperatures – in fact, good vine-growing climate. The Balkan countries, i.e. the more southerly mountainous parts of the Yugoslavian Federation, Bulgaria and the Wallachia plain to the south-east of Romania are subject to a more Mediterranean climate, with higher summer temperatures. Quite small differences in average summer temperatures have a considerable effect on the quality of the wines made from grapes grown in them.

So much then for the bare bones of the lands. I shall, of course, have more to say about them and about the nature of the soils later, when I come to deal with each country individually. Let us put flesh on these bones by considering the inhabitants.

One only has to try to visualise serious-minded, hard-working Czechs, gay waltzing Viennese, fiddling* Magyar gypsies, Montenegrin mountain bandits armed to the teeth, almost oriental Macedonian shepherds tending their sheep as they smoke their hubble-bubbles, to have a vivid, highly romantic and wildly inaccurate picture of what that flesh is like. Their history is so long and eventful that it would take – indeed has taken – many long volumes to cover even the surface of it, and I can do no more here than pick out some highlights that are relevant to the subject of wine-making, however tempting it may be to wander along the many beguiling byways. But there is much literature, and any of my readers who feel encouraged to explore some of the stories of these wonderful lands will find plenty to fascinate them, as I have in writing these pages, especially since so much of the country is now opened up to tourists, and holidays may be spent reasonably cheaply in almost any part of central Europe and the Balkans.

Much of the southern part of the Balkans – Macedonia and the south of what is now Bulgaria and the Dalmatian islands at least – was under the direct influence of Greece at the height of her civilisation. There is ample evidence that it was here that wine-making as we now know it started.

The Romans, first disciples and proselytisers of the Grecian ideals, carried them through Italy into the lands of central Europe, and there is no lack of proof of their thoroughness in all the countries of central and south-eastern Europe. They taught how to select and cultivate the best available types of vines and to make and keep wine. As far as can be surmised from what little evidence there is, the wine that they made would not be acceptable or even perhaps recognisable to us nowadays, but the Romans laid the foundations of the arts that wine-growers and makers the world over practise and try to improve to this day – how best to understand and use one of Nature's greatest gifts to man.

The next landmarks are the Great Migrations of the Turko-Mongolian races during the 6th to 9th centuries, which laid much of the ethnic foundations of the modern eastern European states. Entering Europe from Asia through the so-called Ural-

* It is, regrettably, necessary to note that by 'fiddling' I mean 'violin playing'.

Caspian Gate, these nomadic tribes in their westward flow divided when they met the barrier of the Carpathian mountains, some going north and west into Poland and the Baltic lands, others south and west, up the Danube valley or over the Carpathian passes – the Bulgars, the Magyars, the Avars, the Serbs, the Huns. I find it very difficult to imagine what these migrations must have been like in human terms; nevertheless they happened and the migrants, after periods of marauding and general chaos, eventually settled as they found what they were searching for, bringing their cultures, their languages, their traditions – and their vines – with them. I suppose the nearest modern comparison must be with the great treks of the early American pioneers going west in the last century. An interesting sidelight on one aspect of this huge movement of human cultures in the Dark Ages is that Magyar, the language of the Hungarians, has but one other language remotely like it – Finnish. One can only record but quite fail to imagine the circumstances of the Magyar tribes dividing at the Carpathians, some going northwards to the arctic regions and settling in Finland, while others took the less difficult and shorter paths along the Danube valley and through the mountain passes to help develop one of the most highly individual and intelligent nations in Europe, the Hungarians.

But I must resist the temptation to linger in this extraordinarily interesting part of the establishment of the patterns of European civilisation, and pass on to the next landmarks.

During the period of the Great Migrations and following the decline and defeat of the Romans, many, and highly significant, events to the north and west of Europe culminated in the 8th century in the establishment by Charlemagne of the first glimmerings in western Europe of a civilisation which, as we all know, has rarely reached a state even near to equilibrium up to our own times; and the founding of one of the great factors in the evolution of modern Europe, the Holy Roman Empire, the control of which was to pass a few centuries later to a family of Rhineland landowners whose influence in central Europe is an important part of our story – the Hapsburgs.

The history of the rise of the Hapsburgs in the 13th century, their decline through the 19th century and their fall at the end of the 1914-18 war dominates that long period in this part of

Europe, and the latter part of it at any rate is in the memories, if only vaguely, of most of us. Like many such dynastic empires, its effects on the countries within it were neither wholly good nor wholly bad. As far as we are concerned, it imposed, if only intermittently and partially, some sort of order and regulation over ethnic groups, many of them only too prone to chaos and internecine quarrels.

The Danubian States, throughout their long history, have been the victims of devastating wars and invasions, undoing in a few decades the rewards of centuries of civilising development. The Tartar invasion in the 13th century is an example and after the long and painful rehabilitation following their defeat, the greater disaster of the advance of the Ottoman Turks, which, by the end of the 15th century had engulfed the whole of the Balkan peninsular and, following the defeat of the Hungarian armies at Mohács in 1526, most of Hungary. The tide of invasion was not turned until the Turkish armies were defeated at the gates of Vienna in 1683 and driven back beyond the Hungarian frontiers, not – like the Hapsburgs – to be finally defeated and driven almost out of the Balkans until the 1914-18 war.

The period of Turkish occupation affects the present studies because the Turkish Moslems were forbidden by their religion to drink wine and although wine-making was not completely stopped (in spite of the growers being heavily taxed and otherwise penalised) during what to us seems their generally oppressive and destructive occupation (though by the standards of the times the Turks were in many ways tolerant) viticultural development almost came to a standstill, many vineyards were destroyed and the land was neglected. It is clear, nevertheless, that some of the Turks were assimilated into the countries they had conquered and many of them became sufficiently fond of the habits of western civilisation to appreciate the pleasures of wine drinking (there is a moral to be drawn here), and in a few places wine-making was partially encouraged again; and in those parts of Hungary that were not occupied viticultural development was even accelerated as other sources of good wine disappeared. During this period, too, wine production in Austria increased tremendously – some authorities say tenfold – compared with their size today; but I think this must have included the wine-making areas of what is now Czechoslovakia.

THE LANDS AND THE PEOPLES

The sport of making Turks drunk on wine was a great Viennese joke in the 18th century as, for example, in Mozart's *Entfuhrung auf dem Serail*, composed in 1782, a hundred years after the Siege of Vienna, but at a time when piquant memories of the threat of Turkish occupation and its consequences had been sublimated into a fashionable 'Turkishness' in Austrian art, and incidentally the invention of that masterpiece of the baker's art, that the Viennese call a *kipfel* and the French a *croissant*.

The Prophet specifically forbade the drinking of wine; he could not have forbidden the drinking of spirits as the still was not developed until the 14th century, and no doubt advantage of this useful conscience-salver for alcohol-loving Moslems was taken by the Ottoman Turks, in their occupation of these wine-producing countries (see Appendix 2).

The driving out of the Turkish invaders by the Imperial Austrian armies helped by the Poles under Jan Sobieski consolidated the Hapsburgs' domination of the liberated Danubian States and presaged the full development of their empire, eastward to Transylvania and westward into north-eastern Italy, so that the shape of central Europe was virtually set for another couple of hundred years, in spite of local scraps and revolts, important historically and to the people involved in them, but not affecting greatly the viticultural history of the area. There were, of course, big jobs to be done in clearing up after the devastation left by the retreating Turks, including the replanting of vineyards and the renewing of land left fallow and neglected for a century and a half; and dealing with such minor matters as the advance through Europe of Napoleon Bonaparte, but he loved wine and recorded several that pleased him from Austria and Hungary.

Few of the vineyards of central and south-eastern Europe escaped the disaster of Phylloxera, which swept through Europe from the 1860s onwards, but this will be discussed in the next chapter, which is about the vines.

The 1914-18 war, which brought about the fall of the Hapsburg Empire and the end of the Turkish Sultans, resulted in the reshaping of central and south-eastern Europe into roughly its present form. The breaking up of the Austro-Hungarian Empire made possible the creation of the new state of Czecho-

B

slovakia from Bohemia, Moravia and Slovakia; the creation of Yugoslavia from Slovenia, Serbia, Croatia-Slavonia, Bosnia-Herzegovina, Macedonia and Montenegro; and the enlargement of Romania by the inclusion of Transylvania and Banat within her frontiers. It reduced mighty Austria to a republic, made up of little more than the old Archduchy with Carinthia, Styria and most of the Burgenland; and the ancient kingdom of Hungary to half her former size. And that is how their frontiers remain today, apart from small, more recent variations.

The half century since the signature of the Treaty of Versailles has seen the deposition of Kings, the terror of Nazi Germany encroaching on these new states, and the further devastation of their lands and the enslavement of their peoples in the war of 1939-45. Out of this came the establishment of Socialist republics and the renewed growth of the influence of Russia (she was always interested in this part of Europe) in all except the tiny Austrian republic.

As anyone with the most superficial knowledge of modern history knows, these highly individual peoples have not, under what many would describe as the deadening hand of modern Socialist bureaucracies, lost their strong historical identities and, what is important to us in the present context, they have kept alive and flourishing their great skills as makers of wine, so stubbornly retained through the multiple disasters of their history. We can only most devoutly hope that these clever and industrious peoples will be granted a long period of peaceful progress such as they have so rarely enjoyed in past centuries.

3
THE VINES AND THE WINES

VITIS VINIFERA grows easily and prolifically in most parts of temperate Europe. Indeed, it grows well in the south of England, but it needs the right conditions of weather, aspect* and soil to fruit profitably. As well as that, it needs skill in selection of varieties and cultivation to produce the quality of grapes that can be made into good wine; and, once the grapes have been grown, further perhaps greater skills to make them into good wine.

These further skills, however, while making better wine than would be possible without them from almost any grapes, cannot make fine wines from any but the fruit of the best-grown and best-selected vines. You cannot make a silk purse from a sow's ear.

Therefore, in considering wine-making in any wine-drinking country we must distinguish between the great quantities made from freely fruiting and easily ripened vines for day-to-day consumption primarily at home but latterly for export as well, and the lesser quantities which are cultivated to produce finer

---

* When I use the word 'aspect' in connection with vine growing I mean the physical relationship of the growing vine to the sun; other vines growing with it; the prevailing weather; and generally its physical environment. For example in the northern hemisphere vines planted on south-facing slopes in such a way that each plant has the maximum exposure to the sun's rays are said to grow in a good aspect.

wines. This distinction is important in the present development of the wine trade in all European countries, and, I think, particularly so in the present studies.

Mixed farmers in all vine-growing countries will plant a little bit of land to make wine for themselves and their families, much as an English dairy farmer, for example, will grow small quantities of fruit and vegetables for his own table and, as any good farmer will, market any surplus he may have.

It is unlikely that we shall ever know exactly where grapes were first cultivated and turned into wine. What is sure is that *Vitis vinifera* was well established and flourishing in the countries bordering the Mediterranean many hundreds, perhaps thousands, of years before the Christian era. One of the first full accounts of organised wine-making is in the writings of Mago of Carthage who lived about 550 B.C. and he was clearly writing of well-understood and established practices.

It is equally certain that the Romans taught the arts of vine-growing and wine-making wherever they spread their civilising influence into Europe, and there is abundant evidence of this in artifacts of many kinds found all over the area we are considering, and that, even earlier, the Greeks originated the commercial organisation and marketing of wine, possibly in ancient Thrace, part of which is in modern Bulgaria. So it is fair to say that we are dealing with the very heart of the development of wine-making in the western world.

Very little is known of how the countless variations of *V. vinifera* developed and were discarded or encouraged over the centuries; and it is only in comparatively recent times that the most successful varieties have been 'fixed' and, indeed, improved by vegetative propagation. Cyrus Redding, writing in 1833, and one of the earliest English scholarly authorities on the subject, writes:

The French, who understand the culture of the vine better than any other people, say, that the art of adapting each particular species of the vine to the soil most congenial to its culture is yet in its infancy.

I cannot be sure of this, but it seems a good guess that a lot was learned about this important part of viticulture after the scourge of Phylloxera struck European vineyards in the 1860s and '70s.

THE VINES AND THE WINES 21

Phylloxera is an aphid that destroys vines by sucking their roots. It is native to the United States east of the Rocky Mountains and was unknown in Europe before some American vines were imported into France in the 1850s and '60s, but it is so virulent and the European environment suited it so well that before the end of the nineteenth century three-quarters of French vines had been destroyed and Phylloxera had spread all over Europe. Some authorities have claimed that it was introduced into the vineyards of California by vine cuttings imported there from France – poetic justice indeed! True or not, Phylloxera was eventually brought under control by the grafting of scions (or buds) of *V. vinifera* on to rootstocks of American species resistant to it, and that is how most *V. vinifera* is grown today. There are a few exceptions that we will deal with later.

Parenthetically, this may be the place to clear up something that has puzzled many students: what are 'hybrids', and why are they so much frowned upon in France and other serious wine-making countries?

In this context, hybrids are not the results of natural cross-fertilisation between varieties of the species *V. vinifera*; after all, most of the enormous number of these varieties must ultimately have been the result of such hybridisations over the centuries; nor are they the more recent artificial hybridisations of which obvious examples are the Riesling/Sylvaner crosses such as Müller-Thurgau and Scheurebe. The hybrids that the French and others forbid in certain circumstances for wine-making are those between different species of the genus *Vitis*, usually between *V. vinifera* and one of the American species, e.g. *V. riparia* or *V. rupestris,* which provide root stocks for the grafting of *V. vinifera*, the idea of the hybridisations being to combine the quality of *V. vinifera* with the vigour, disease-resistance and fecundity of the imported species. We must be clear that hybridisation (the breeding of new kinds by cross-fertilisation) is not the same as the grafting of one species on to the root stock of another. This is common practice with commercial fruit-growing nowadays.

Much work in the field of hybridising between species has been and is being done in Europe and the USA, and no doubt quite acceptably for grapes grown for purposes other than wine-making. Wines made from grapes grown on American hybrid vines are, to most palates, unpleasant in flavour and are readily distinguished by the modern techniques of chromatography. Any readers wishing to go more deeply into this subject will find A. J. Winkler's *General Viticulture* most informative. American scholarship in this field is very sound and Winkler's book is comprehensive. (See Appendix 5.)

As we shall see, all the countries of central and south-eastern Europe have their own native varieties of *V. vinifera*, and this is complicated by the fact that many of the migrating peoples and other settlers brought their vines with them, and many of these are well established. Good examples are the Furmint which was brought into Hungary by Walloon settlers from the Low Countries, and Ezerjo, grown in several south-eastern countries, which is believed to have originated in India. I will deal with these native varieties in detail as each country is considered separately.

Another fact that must have been fundamental to the extraordinary growth of vine cultivation for making wine over the centuries (apart from the obvious delight that our forefathers found in discovering the beneficent effects of alcohol) is that vines produce the sort of grapes that make good wine best on land that would be regarded as poor for most other crops; and conversely on land that would be considered good for most purposes of cultivation, the vine will produce grapes that are of little use for making good wine. Suppose all the vines in the Médoc, the Côte d'Or or the Tokaj-Hegyalja district were to be grubbed up and the land ploughed – a frightful nightmare! – the fact is that there is not much else that could be profitably grown on it. I have not seen this point made in these terms elsewhere in my fairly extensive reading on the subject, but it seems to demonstrate one of the merciful dispensations of Providence, or Nature's wonderful economy in creation, whichever way you like to look at it.

In very general terms, the traditions, lands and climates of central Europe – Austria, Czechoslovakia, Hungary, Slovenia and Transylvania – are especially well suited to the making of white wines, while those of the Balkan countries are better suited, particularly because of the higher average temperatures, to the making of red wines; white wines made in these warmer, more southerly conditions tend to lack the qualities of freshness and acidity that are the essential parts of the attractiveness of white wines. 70 per cent of Hungarian production and about 85 per cent of Austrian is of white wines, but even so, the best red wines are still made in the area of the old kingdom of Hungary, and some of them are very fine.

Let us, therefore, first consider the white wine vines, and of these the most important is *Riesling*. It is interesting to note that Riesling is the only vine name that is known and remembered by consumers in the British Isles. I suppose this is because it makes the kind of white wine that we like to drink, and we learned to acquire that taste from the success here in the immediate postwar years of the excellent Slovenian Riesling, better known here as 'Lutomer Riesling'; but remember that wine labelled 'Yugoslavian Riesling' is unlikely to have come from Lutomer or even from Slovenia and may not be of such high quality. Yugoslavia is a big country, with a wide variety of terrain and climate as I shall show. I believe Lutomer Riesling to have been the first widely-distributed wine to be labelled with a place- and grape-name in this way, Lutomer being the area in eastern Slovenia where the grapes are grown. This excellent practice of describing a wine by place- and grape-names is in accordance with regulations formulated in Hungary in the 19th century and only practised elsewhere at that time, and then only partially, in Germany. Now, of course, it is becoming much more widely used in all parts of the world.

There are two versions of the Riesling vine, one originating (and identified very early) in the Rhineland of Germany, and the other in France. Both have a number of synonyms (some of which I will list later) but for now I will refer to them as *Rhineriesling* and *Wälschriesling* respectively.

Rhineriesling, as we know, grown in its native conditions on the Rhine and Moselle, makes some of the finest white wines in the world, which reach the highest levels of excellence. It makes these wines in the difficult conditions of soil and climate at the northern limit in Germany of European vine cultivation, thus – as happens so often with very fine wines – giving of its best where it has to struggle almost for existence. *Rhineriesling* is fairly prolific but it buds and ripens late, needing every hour of sunshine in its growing season. Many attempts have been made – and are still being made – in Germany by crossing it with earlier-budding and ripening vines, like *Sylvaner*, to produce a more easy-to-grow hybrid of *Rhineriesling* quality. Some of these are well-established, but none have achieved the impossible task of producing qualities that are in themselves the result of the native difficulties of the *Rhineriesling* vine: and this is proved, if proof were needed, by the fact that, grown in easier climates (and it has been planted all over the world) where there are no ripening difficulties, even on similar soils and in similar aspects, *Rhineriesling* does not make wine that approaches the qualities of bouquet and flavour that at its best it gives in its native Rhineland. *Rhineriesling* is grown in the countries we are considering, particularly in Austria, but the wine made from it, while possessing some of the intrinsic fine qualities of the vine, tends to be a little dull, lacking freshness and a proper balancing acidity; in fact what in the wine trade we call a little 'flabby'. Its cousin *Wälschriesling* is the characteristic Riesling of this part of Europe and is far more extensively planted. *Wälschriesling* has the readily distinguishable Riesling qualities of flavour, and rather less of bouquet, and although never achieving the greatest heights of excellence attained by its German cousin growing in the best of its native soils and aspects, it nevertheless makes excellent, well-balanced wine.

The distinguishing of one from another of the endless varieties of *V. vinifera* is properly work for the botanists, who look for such things as leaf shapes and growing habits. I mention this because, in a booklet published in 1967 at the famous Wine Institute in Geisenheim, *Der Riesling und seine Weine*, the authors go to some lengths to prove by these botanists' criteria that *Wälschriesling* is a 'false' Riesling. The booklet is a very full study of all aspects of the Riesling vine and I hope it may be translated and made generally available, but one has the feeling that the Germans go to quite extraordinary lengths to prove that the two vines are different. Methinks they do protest too much! We, who judge these things organoleptically – or, as I prefer to put it, by our noses and palates – can have no doubt that the two vines are closely related. The excellent French authorities L. Portés and Ruyssen distinguish between the two vines and give France as the country of origin of *Wälschriesling*; the Geisenheim booklet is more specific and mentions Champagne. It is strange therefore that it is often called 'Italian' Riesling and one can only suppose that it found its ideal terrain in north-east Italy and central Europe quite early, for it has grown there for hundreds of years.

Here are some of the more common synonyms for both these vines:

RHINERIESLING: *Weisser Riesling, Rössling, Moselriesling, Niederlander, Klingelberger, Kleinriesling, Pfeffel, Gentil Aromatique* (France), *Riesling Renano* (Italy), *Ryzlink Rynsky* (Czechoslovakia), *Renski Riesling, Rajnski Rizling* (Yugoslavia), *Rajnai Rizling* (Hungary).
WÄLSCHRIESLING: *Welschriesling, Italian Riesling, Olasz Riesling* (Hungary), *Laski Riesling, Grasevina, Grasica* (Yugoslavia).

A list of other well-distributed white wine grapes grown in central and south-eastern Europe must start with *Sylvaner*, an easy-growing, fairly disease-free, early ripening vine, producing pleasant, light, refreshing wines of no great distinction. *Sylvaner* is grown more or less extensively in all the countries in this area. Partly because it is so accommodating and well-behaved a vine, it has been used as one of the parents in the many Riesling hybrids, the best known being *Müller-Thurgau*, much grown in Germany and Austria, a little in Yugoslavia, but not, to my knowledge, elsewhere. The results of hybridisations are unpredictable (we all know how sceptical George Bernard Shaw was of the virtues of the hybrid from his remark to Isadora Duncan: '. . . but suppose the child were born with my body and your brains!'). This sort of thing happens, and instead of the result of the cross-breeding being the best it may well combine the least desirable characteristics of both parents or even result in something outrageously different. I think few would claim *Müller-Thurgau* to be anything like Riesling or even much of an improvement on Sylvaner.

Another vine from the German rather than the French tradition grown in most of our countries is *Traminer,* with its strong and characteristic bouquet and taste, comparable in its assertiveness with the vast Muscat family, to which I have often thought it may be related. Both grape varieties have the characteristic, by no means universal, that the flavour and aroma of the fresh ripe grape are carried through into the finished wine. The Muscat variety that is grown in all parts of central and south-eastern Europe is *Muskat Ottonel*. I have not tasted wine made from this grape in all our countries, but the one made in Romania I find to be excellent and beautifully made. I think it is a pity that there is not at present in Great Britain much more discrimination of quality among the drinkers of sweet white wines. This is regarded as a taste to be ashamed of and unfashionable, which is absurd. When the fashion changes, then the wines made in central and south-eastern Europe *Muskat Ottonel* will come into their own. As it is, our loss is Russia's gain – they love these sweet, full-flavoured white wines.

In the French tradition, all the members of the noble Pinot family grow well. *Pinot Gris*, which in Hungary is called *Szürkebarát*, meaning, I do not know why, 'Grey Friar', and in Germany and Austria *Ruländer,* is well established everywhere. It is interesting to note that in Alsace and Switzerland it is called 'Tokay' which is odd because its wine in no way resembles the great Tokaji wine of Hungary.* *Pinot Blanc*, usually known by its German name of *Weissburgunder,* makes good wine in Austria, and its near relation *Chardonnay* flourishes as far south as Bulgaria, where it has been extensively planted. To complete the Pinot picture, *Pinot Noir (Blauburgunder)* is grown in all parts but as far as I know it is always vinified to make red wine, the quality of which varies greatly, but reaches really typical quality in the Villány district in south-west Hungary.

Continuing with the French white wine vines, *Sauvignon* is grown successfully in Hungary, Romania and Yugoslavia, where it produces good typical, usually sweetish wine resembling more the Sauvignon of Bordeaux than the very different styles made from it in the Loire Valley. Its partner, *Sémillon*, is grown in Slovenia and Macedonia in Yugoslavia.

This may be the place to mention that in central and south-eastern Europe there are formidable language problems and, although I have asked many questions and received interesting and sometimes surprising answers, I cannot be sure that some of

* There is similarly the 'Tocai' of north-eastern Italy.

THE VINES AND THE WINES 27

the so-called 'native' vines whose names we shall come to as we deal with each country in turn are not familiar old friends masquerading under other names. I have tried to avoid guessing and have given translations only where I feel reasonably sure that the information I have is correct.

Before we go on to the red wine producing grapes, I should mention one other white grape which belongs to central and south-eastern Europe – *Furmint*. This vine was first introduced into the Tokaji district of Hungary after the Tartar invasion of 1241 by King Bela IV, who invited Walloon wine-growers to settle in the depopulated areas, and they brought this vine with them. It produces wine which was called 'froment' probably because its pleasant yellow colour resembles ripening wheat, and this was Magyar-ised into its present name. There is no doubt that *Furmint* is a 'noble' vine and, in conditions that suit it, produces most distinctive wine with high extract (we will consider the meaning of extract a little later). It is grown in all parts of south-eastern Europe and in Germany and Italy.

The characteristic red wine grape of the whole of central and south-eastern Europe is *Kadarka*. It takes its name from the ancient Albanian town of Skardarka (now Skutari) where it is supposed to have originated, but it makes the best wines when grown in Hungary and Yugoslavia. It is one of the varieties producing the legendary 'Bull's Blood' of Eger.

In this part of Europe two basic styles of red wine are recognised, the so-called 'Siller', rather more like a rosé but traditionally deeper in colour than the rosé wines we are used to, made by taking the must off the skins after only a few days. In this way the vinification is easier and the wine drinkable much more quickly. The other basic style produces the deeper, heavier red wines where the must ferments out on the skins, drawing from them all that they have to give. I will consider this a little more when, at the end of this chapter, I discuss developments in wine-making. There are of course many gradations of this technique of red-wine-making; some light rosé wines are made nowadays in most wine-producing countries. That made from Kadarka is pleasant and has the typical slightly aromatic flavour of this grape.

Other than Kadarka and some purely local varieties which we will mention when we come to them, most red wine is made from the classic French noble vines. *Pinot Noir* (*Blauburgunder* in Austria, *Nágyburgundi* in Hungary) is extensively planted in most of our countries and, well grown in soils and aspects that suit it, produces wine with the unmistakable Pinot bouquet and flavour.

I am not going to fall into the trap of trying to put the subtleties of wine-tasting into words; you either know what particular wines taste and smell like or, if you do not, the only way to learn is by drinking them and cultivating a 'taste memory'. In my experience, certain grapes make wine with such distinctive taste and aroma qualities as to be readily identifiable: Traminer and the Muscats, of course, but to me Pinot Noir is another and so is Riesling. But having written this, I must record that the late Allen Sichel once told me that if he had a pound for every occasion when he had mistaken Claret for Burgundy and vice versa, he would have been a rich man – and I surely need not add that his palate was excellent and highly trained, in fact one of the best of his generation.

The other Burgundy grape – *Gamay* (*Blaufrankischer* in Austria, *Kékfrankos* in Hungary) is grown in those two countries and in Yugoslavia, making excellent wines, particularly in the area around Sopron and the Burgenland; not, at any rate to me, a grape as easy to identify from its wine as Pinot Noir, even when grown in Burgundy.

The great Bordeaux cépages are grown in all parts of our area, *Cabernet Franc* and *Cabernet-Sauvignon* in Slovenia and the Balkan countries and *Merlot* (*Médoc Noir*) in Hungary, most parts of the Yugoslavian Federation and Romania. I cannot claim to have tasted wines made from these grapes in all the countries that grow them, but those I have tasted, while good sound wines, do not seem to have the qualities that one expects from one's experience of Claret, but that is, I suppose, expecting too much of them.

Here and there *Blue Portuguese* is grown and, as one would expect, makes big, deep-coloured wines, but of no great quality. I have been unable to discover which of the many Portuguese varieties it is; in fact some authorities claim that it is native to Austria and has nothing to do with Portugal.

The Italian *Barbera* is grown in Slovenia and in the Istrian Peninsular, which is not surprising, as Italian traditions are naturally strong in these parts, and I have no doubt other Italian varieties are to be found there. Other red wine varieties abound in the Balkan countries and will be mentioned when we come to them in dealing with the individual countries.

I will round off this chapter with some general thoughts about wine making, how it is developing in all parts of Europe nowadays, and some prognostications about the future.

We have been so spoiled for so long with notions of 'fine wines of great vintages' – or illusions of them – that we easily forget that over ninety per cent (perhaps as much as ninety-nine per cent) of the world's wines are nothing of the kind; and are none the worse for it.

Nor, as far too many people appear to think is necessary, can all the wine we drink be simply split between 'fine wines' and 'plonk' (a word I will not use again). Apart from the evidence of stupid snobbishness, it is not as simple as that. Concepts of wine-making are changing and knowledge of the details of all the processes connected with it have so increased in the past half century (and in fairness I must add that much of this knowledge explains and helps to ease the application of processes known if not always understood by wine makers all over the world for centuries) that many assumptions and preconceptions are having to be swept away and a fresh look taken at the whole subject. In other words, many of us must stop kidding ourselves.

Many of the preconceptions among British wine lovers particularly have been encouraged by what Cyril Ray has aptly called 'the baroque school' of writers about wine, founded by Professor George Saintsbury and elaborated by other literary figures of more or less distinction to create a considerable body of work, remarkable, and often delightful, for its witty, allusive style, but supporting a romantic approach to wine that I believe has done more harm than good, to the extent that honest, very pleasant little wines have to be garnished with proud names and famous vintages before the public will deign to drink them.

Mainly by accidents of geography and history, we, in Great Britain, have always looked mostly to France and Germany for our table wines and I am not such a partisan as to deny that there are some quite superb wines – the finest there are – made in, for example, Bordeaux, Burgundy and parts of the Rhine and Moselle valleys, but the economics of the making and bringing to maturity of such wines, the world-wide demand for them and their scarcity, have put them out of reach of all but the rich, and few of us are lucky enough to taste wine of this quality more than a few times in a lifetime. The fact that such wines exist and will continue to be made does not mean that every *crû classé* and *petit château* in Bordeaux, every *crû* and, indeed, *commune* in the Côte d'Or, or all the growths in the Rheingau and Middle Moselle are, by their own qualities, entitled to profit from their reflected glory, to the extent that many of them create demands and command prices that are out of any relation to their intrinsic worth. The Burgundians knew full well what they were doing when they tacked the names of their best vineyards to the names of communes, so that Gevrey took on Chambertin, Chambolle took on Musigny and so on, to their greater glory – and commercial value – to this day!

In France this position has been encouraged by the rough-riding operation of her laws of controlled appellation, and this, it cannot be denied, to the profit of growers and négociarts. But several factors, not least the greater and faster spread of knowledge that I mentioned earlier, and the necessities of agricultural regulation essential to the working of the European Community, have made it possible and necessary to look more closely at the factors controlling the quality of wine. This unromantic approach will take a bit of swallowing by certain sections of the public, who will have to accept facts that may at first upset their comfortable assumptions, and by the wine-growing countries whose lesser growths profit so greatly from the reputations of their finest products; but it will oblige them eventually to put their houses in order and can only be good in the long run for wine drinkers everywhere.

Given the all-important facts of the variety of vine planted and its age, the nature of the soil and subsoil, the weather, and the aspect of the vineyard, the quality of a wine can be controlled at the growing stage by the skill with which the vines are tended and, above all, trained and pruned, and the timing of the picking and pressing of the grapes. After that, every process directly affects the quality of the finished wine. These factors are common to all wines from Chateau Lafite down to the humblest Balkan peasant wine.

While the grapes are growing, they acquire their qualities mainly by the natural process known as photosynthesis through the action of light on the leaves and to a lesser extent the berries; and by the absorption of water and elements in solution in water, through the roots. The photosynthesis produces the grape sugar, which in its turn helps to provide many of the other complex components, including tannin, and is therefore of primary importance, but little or nothing can be done to control it. Nature will see to it, if the vines are healthy and well cultivated, that enough leaves grow to do their necessary work. The subtler qualities of the wine, however, are believed to come from the elements taken from the subsoil by the root system, and depending on how the vine is pruned, these elements are distributed in a greater or lesser degree among the fruit that the vine has been pruned to bear. These elements can be determined by chemical analysis of the finished wine and are known as 'the extract'. It is generally agreed that the ultimate quality of the wine is determined by the nature and quantity of this extract. (Again there is nothing new about this – we just know rather more about it.) As the effect of the extract on the finished wine takes time, it is an acceptable rule that the higher the extract, the longer the time the wine will need to reach full maturity. Perhaps I should make it clear here that tannin is not part of the extract but helps in the long and complex process of wine maturation; it is not in itself an important element of quality.

It follows, therefore, that if it is intended that the wine is to be for drinking soon after it has been made, the presence of too much extract will be a handicap. Therefore the vines in this instance will be pruned to produce more fruit, with a consequently smaller share of the elements forming the extract. In recent international discussions and studies about wine qualities, a case has been made for the classification of these qualities in the sense of whether they are for quick consumption or for keeping to mature, by the measurement of the extract in them. This, then, is the first important factor controlling wine quality – extract.

Once the grapes have been picked (and the judgment of the best time to pick them is obviously very important), every process affects quality; but the two most important things that concern us now are the control of the first fermentation and, in the case of red wines particularly, the length of time that the skins, pulp and pips are kept in the fermenting must. It is necessary for the must to reach a certain temperature before the fermentation can start. The temperature will rise as the fermentation gets under way and if it becomes too high and the fermentation consequently becomes too violent and out of control, the wine will spoil. This has always been recognised by wine makers as one of the most critical parts of the process, but it is only in recent years that suitable cooling apparatus has been devised so that the temperature of the fermenting must can be controlled and the process slowed down or even stopped, as required. Thus fermentation may be stopped while there remains fermentable sugar in the must. Many a good wine – indeed some of the very greatest – has been ruined in the past by uncontrolled, violent overheated fermentation. It is clear from this that the ability to control or stop fermentation is an important factor in the determination of quality.

The other factor is equally important and applies particularly to red wine – the length of time that the must is allowed to stay in contact with the skins, pulp, pips and other lesser solids that remain after pressing. At one extreme we have the few hours needed to give a little colour to a rosé wine, and at the other, the leaving of it in the must until the primary fermentation stops in up to three or four weeks, and all that can be has been taken from the solids. Now it is clear that in the second of these extremes, the wine will need a long time, first in cask and then in bottle to become drinkable, say a minimum of two and a half years, while in the first, and also with most white wines, the wine will be ready to drink often as soon as four months after the vintage. Between these two extremes there are, naturally, infinite gradations. The second extreme usually applies to the great red wines because they can be sold for prices that enable their makers to give them this time, but most red wines all over the world including many in Bordeaux and Burgundy nowadays are made by the quicker maturing methods, so that less tannin and extract is in the finished wine and it is therefore ready to drink very much more quickly.

I have made this point about the great French wines, not to denigrate them, but to bring them down to the necessary perfectly valid comparison with many of their cousins made in the central and south-eastern European wine areas, where exactly the same problems exist and are as thoroughly understood.

So in the future we shall have more wine, some of which will perhaps not be as fine as it is capable of being if expense did not matter, but nevertheless made at a reasonable cost and capable of being drunk with pleasure much sooner after the grapes are gathered. Some merchants like to call these wines 'commercial' which to me does not seem fair, as the finer wines are equally 'commercial', as I understand the meaning of the word, but I suppose we cannot expect the 'baroque' or 'romantic' attitude to disappear overnight.

Of course, in writing these notes I have enormously simplified my description of the processes of wine-making, but I have tried to show the essentials in sufficient detail to support the points I have been making.

It may be argued that these facts represent a levelling in wine qualities, and to the extent that probably less very fine wine is now being made, this is true. But against this I have no doubt that the overwhelming improvements in the availability of good wines from all wine-making countries, the sort of wine that we can all afford to enjoy, is ample compensation. In the context of this book, I hope it will encourage wine drinkers to explore and, I suggest, take more seriously the many excellent wines produced in the countries of central and south-eastern Europe, which we will now proceed to examine in greater detail.

4
AUSTRIA
(Österreich)

A Republic
Area: *83,000 square kilometres.* Population: *7,300,000*

I MUST resist the temptation to write about this beautiful little country, half the size of England and Wales, in the terms of a travel book. In Vienna, capital of the Hapsburg Emperors, pushed into her extreme eastern lands, Austria possesses what is to me the brightest jewel among European capitals; and out of her truncated, apparently unbalanced land surface she has fashioned an economy and way of life that work, and give her a modest prosperity and stability: and this without nostalgia and falling back entirely on the capital of her rich tradition of history and in the arts and literature. Austria is a Catholic country, and in her south-eastern wine-growing lands enjoys the so-called Pannonian climate system, combining the best of the northern and southern European climates – or so they claim. Pannonia was the Roman province covering the south-east of Austria.

Most of the land surface of Austria consists of mountainous country and only the low hills, foothills and plains to the extreme north-east, east and south-east, bordering on Czechoslovakia, Hungary and Slovenia are suitable for the growing of grapes, but much of this land has as long a history of wine-making as any in Europe.

The Austrians are a wine-drinking people, increasingly so, with an annual consumption in 1969 of 35 litres per head, which is rather more than Austria produces in a normal year at present; in fact until quite recently she had not been an important wine-exporting country, and her biggest customer was her neighbour West Germany. However, now that she takes her wine-making more seriously, she has increased the efficiency of her cultivation and vinification and the area planted with vines, so that her annual production has trebled over the past ten years. In the excellent 1970 vintage it reached the record figure of three million hectolitres; and in that year the proportion of white wine to red was 89% to 11% which is what it has been roughly for a long time, although the proportion of red wine will tend to increase a little, I think, in the future.

It is difficult to know from import statistics quite how much of her export is of her own production and how much wine imported from her neighbours, including Italy and even Spain, and blended with her own. Some of the Empress Maria Theresa's regulations deal with this function of historical Austria as a kind of clearing house for European wines. These things die hard! I am assured, however, that serious efforts are being made to prevent the exportation as Austrian wine of any imported wine, and that future statistics will give this distinction. And to be fair to the Austrians, they cannot be blamed if the bureaucrats who keep statistics are more interested in the countries from which wines are imported – never mind who made them.

In 1970, 17,300 hectolitres of wine from Austria were imported into Great Britain, about equally divided between red and rosé, and white.

I am indebted for most of the information I have about the wines of this country to the Austrian Wine Institute, which was formed in 1968 with Government encouragement, from representatives of production and distribution organisations and the rump of a previous, less comprehensive organisation, for the purposes of putting their house in order, controlling the quality of Austrian wines and publicising them internationally. I am bound to say that I think such a body was badly needed, and I wish them success as I would any organisation with such laudable intentions. Many Austrian wines are so good, distinctive and charming in quality that they richly deserve to be protected and their purity of style preserved.

It is interesting to note, incidentally, that the distinction I tried to make clear at the end of my chapter 'The vines and the wines' is recognised in Austria by distinguishing between high quality – *Spitzenweine** – and the more general – *Tischweine* (table wines).

A method of vine-growing has been developed in Austria and is used also in other European vine-growing countries, by one of her most respected merchants, Lenz Moser, and it is named after him. Briefly, it consists of growing each vine separately with space around it, rather than in closely planted rows as is normal. By this method it is claimed that there is a considerable saving in labour costs without deterioration of quality (see Appendix 3).

Austrian wines are labelled rather like those of her West German neighbours, with a place-name, either of an area as Wachauer, or of a town as Gumpoldskirchener (-*er* being the possessive suffix), and a grape-name, or sometimes with just a grape-name. They will sometimes state whether the wine is unsugared – *naturrein* or *naturbellasen* – and with the improved regulation of her wine production this is likely to become more important, although with her warmer climate the addition of sugar is much less often needed than it is in Germany. Similarly 'spätlese' has rather less significance here than in Germany; vintages can easily and much more safely be deferred here, with the long, warm autumns and the late incidence of frost. Occasionally they produce an 'ice wine'. The alcoholic strength of Austrian wines is higher than German wines, being usually between 11.5° and 12.5° G.L.

That remarkable woman, the Empress Maria Theresa, revised the Austrian wine laws in 1780 and it is extraordinary that many of her regulations are still in operation, as I mentioned earlier and, as I shall show, those governing the *heurigen*.

The total area of wine cultivation in Austria is recorded in 1969 as 46,920 hectares and this is divided by law into regions and sub-divided as follows:

LOWER AUSTRIA (*Niederösterreich*) – *29,074 hectares, 62% of total.*
Wachau, Krems, Langenlois, Weinviertel, Donauland, Baden, Vöslau.

---

* One hopes that the Austrian Wine Institute, in the process of putting their house in order, will see that this *cachet* is only allowed for wines worthy of it.

AUSTRIA

BURGENLAND – *14,883 hectares, 31.7% of total.*
Rust, Neusiedlersee, Eisenberg.
STYRIA (*Steiermark*) – *2,139 hectares, 4.6% of total.*
Südsteiermark, Klöch-Oststeiermark, Weststeiermark.
VIENNA (*Wien*) – *797 hectares, 1.7% of total.*
Negligible areas in other parts totalling 25 hectares.

There are in all about 72,000 agricultural holdings in Austria cultivating vines, but of these only 39,000 are wholly engaged in growing grapes for wine, mostly in fairly small units of between 5 and 20 hectares.

THE VINES

By far the most widely planted white wine vine in Austria is her characteristic *Grüner Veltliner* (*grüner* means *green*), which accounts for 23% of all she produces and that largely in Lower Austria. A similar vine is grown, I believe, in Italy, and a little is grown in Austria of a close relation named *Frühroter Veltliner* (and I assume that *frühroter* means an early-ripening red grape); but *Grüner Veltliner* is as typically Austrian as *Rhineriesling* is German and *Furmint* Hungarian, and Austria is rightly very proud of the wines made from it, which have a delicate though pronounced characteristic flavour and aroma, and I find it unique. If it has a fault it is in a tendency to be a little lacking in acidity, but this may be due more to the influence of climate and perhaps methods of vinification – or even the Austrian taste – than to a fault in the grape itself; and it is often '*spritzig*' (the French call it *pétillant* and the Italians *frizzante*) which means that a little carbon dioxide gas, the product of fermentation, remains in the wine, giving it a faint prickle on the tongue.

Other white wine grapes which I believe are native to Austria are *Neuburger*, producing 4.1% of her output, the *Zierfandler* or *Spätrot* (as *früh* means *early*, *spät* means *late*), which with *Rotgipfler*, a red grape, makes what is Austria's best-known wine, Gumpoldskirchener; and a vine called *Bouvier* or *Bouviertraube* which, I believe, is the subject of experiments and is certainly grown in Yugoslavia.

These are the native types, but *Wälschriesling* and the Riesling/Sylvaner hybrid *Müller-Thurgau* each produce over

9% of Austria's wine production. The remaining white wine grapes are *Pinot Blanc* (*Weisser Burgunder* or *Klevner*), *Pinot Gris* (*Ruländer*) *Rhineriesling*, *Traminer* and *Muskat Ottonel*.

The principal vines used for Austria's small red wine production are *Blue Portuguese* (*Blauer Portugieser*) (which according to some authorities may be native to Austria and nothing to do with Portugal) making 4.3%, *Gamay* (*Blaufrankisch*) making 4% (and remember that this 8.3% is of a total red wine production of only about 11%) with the small balance covered by *St Laurent* (a red Muskat), *Pinot Noir* (*Blauer Burgunder*), *Rotgipfler* mentioned above, a purely native vine called *Blauer Wildbacher* grown only in a small part of Styria, and again a vine about which I know little, *Zweigelt*, which I assume is native to Austria, and like the *Bouvier* is being experimented with there.

I will now deal with each of the four regions fairly briefly, starting with the biggest, making nearly two-thirds of Austria's whole production.

Lower Austria (Niederösterreich)

This could be called the 'north-east corner' of Austria. It contains the majority of the population and borders on Bohemia and Moravia in Czechoslovakia to the north and east, and to the west running into the foothills of the Alps and the Bayerische Wald, and limited to the south and south-east by the borders of the Burgenland and Styrian regions, bisected by the Danube and, of course, containing Vienna. It has a surprising variety of climate, soils (including old rocks, gravel, sand, loess and even chalky loam) and type of country, and produces most of Austria's best wines – certainly her best white wines. It is by law divided into seven districts as follows, starting from the west.

Lower Austria: Wachau   The valley of the Danube, between the Dunkelsteiner Forest on the south and the Bohemian Massif on the north, and west of Stein (where the district of Krems begins) is a beautiful part of the country, where the vineyards are terraced on quite steep slopes, much as they are on parts of the Rhine and Moselle. The terraced vineyards on subsoils of gneiss and schist (see Appendix 1 on soil types) are planted with *Grüner Veltliner* and *Rhineriesling*, producing high quality wines of

AUSTRIA

pronounced bouquet and flavour; and on the higher slopes, the sweeter aromatic *Muskat-Ottonel* is grown. Lower down the Danube with a loess soil, the shallower, lower terraces are planted with *Neuburger* and *Müller-Thurgau*. The finest wines of Wachau are from Spitz, Loiben, Dürnstein and Weissenkirchen, all names to look for on Austrian wine bottles.

Lower Austria: Krems This district runs east from the Wachau wine district and differs from it in that at this point the Danube valley widens and flattens. It is centred round the historic town of Krems. Viticulture in the district flourished as far back as A.D. 450 and was encouraged by the Church under one of those autocratic bishoprics which, whatever they may have done for Christianity, certainly helped greatly in the development of vine-growing and wine-making, to the glory of God and their own tables. *Grüner Veltliner* grows well here on the loess, and *Rhine-riesling* makes a good typical fruity wine. *Neuburger* and *Müller-Thurgau* are also grown. Krems wines have a reputation for high quality.

Lower Austria: Langenlois East of Krems, the river Kamp runs into the Danube from the north, and on the slopes of the Kamptal, in delightful country, is the district named after the large town of Langenlois with its surrounding 100 hectares of vineyards. The district is described as of 'manifold soils' and the vine has flourished there for centuries. Names to look for are Schönberg, Strass, Zöbing, and again *Grüner Veltliner, Rhine-riesling, Neuburger* and *Müller-Thurgau* are the vines grown.

Lower Austria: Weinviertel (literally 'wine quarter') This is by far the largest of the Lower Austrian wine districts. It is a wide stretch of fairly flat land, running from Manhartsberg in the west right across the north, bounded by the frontier with Moravia to the March (the frontier with Slovakia) in the east, and to the Danube in the south as far west as the Krems district. It is a rich land of mixed agriculture, vineyards on gentle hills on a variety of soils, growing the ubiquitous *Grüner Veltliner, Weisser Burgunder, Traminer* and *Müller-Thurgau*; alternating with wheatfields and including important wine centres, to the north around the towns of Röschitz, Pulkau and Retz, making good *Grüner Veltliner* wine in the local warm climate. Retz is a beautiful old wine town, with labyrinthine cellars and ancient traditions of wine-making. Haugsdorf in the Pulkautal has a reputation for making a strong red wine, I think from the *Blau Portugieser*. South from Haugsdorf we come to the Ravelsbach district, between the valleys of the Kamp and the Schmida – a highly reputed area for spritzig *Grüner Veltliner* and *Müller-Thurgau*: then south to the stretch of the Danube known as Am Wagram (not the Wagram that every schoolboy knows – that is the other side of Vienna). Am Wagram is the northern extent of the Tullnerfeld, where there are loess terraces and stony soils, rather like the Krems area, fertile lands producing excellent wines. This part is called the Upper Weinviertel; the Lower Weinviertel runs from Falkenstein and Poysdorf in the north, down through Zistersdorf and Matzen to Wolkersdorf just north of Vienna. This is some of Austria's richest agricultural land, growing corn and market garden produce – and incidentally supplying, I am told, Austria's needs in petroleum, as well as vines. Falkenstein and Poysdorf have historical reputations for fine wines, and supplied the many great houses of the district, the Grand- and Archducal courts and customers as far afield as the Russian Tsars in St Petersburg. The Weinviertel, and particularly the lower part of it, is clearly an important part of Austria, land of many battles, with the roads connecting the Imperial Court with Prague, Brünn (now Brno) and the western lands running through it; good hunting country around the many noblemen's seats; and now, riches upon riches, petroleum!

Lower Austria: Donauland   A narrow strip of land between the south bank of the Danube and the Wienerwald (a range of wooded hills south-west of Vienna and running up to the suburbs of that city – in fact the Vienna Woods where the Tales come from), the Leithagebirge, with the old city of Klosterneuberg, home of the Austrian Wine Research Centre; to the east and westward Traismauer and Prellenkirchen. One of the oldest wine-producing areas of Austria and growing the usual *Grüner Veltliner*, *Rhineriesling*, *Müller-Thurgau*, *Weisser Burgunder* and *Traminer*.

Lower Austria: Baden   To the east of the Donauland on the

AUSTRIA

heavy limestone and gravel soil on the eastern slopes of the Wienerwald and enjoying a particularly warm and dry climate, this is the area of Gumpoldskirchen and the two native vines, *Spätrot* and *Rotgipfler* from which its wine is made. It is probably the best-known (if not the best) Austrian white wine. It is full-flavoured, usually sweetish and alcoholically strong, with in good vintages nice balancing acidity. 'Gumpoldskirchener' stands in some danger of becoming the 'Liebfraumilch' of Austria, but the Wine Institute will, I am sure, guard against the danger of its prostitution; it has special qualities which are well worth preserving, and make it one of the outstanding wines of central Europe. Other good white wines are made in this area from the towns of Baden, Pfaffstätten and Traiskirchen. Apart from *Spätrot* and *Rotgipfler*, this is the area for the other Austrian native vine, *Neuburger*. Perchtoldsdorf is a popular centre for 'Heurigen' which I will mention when we deal with Vienna, to which it really belongs.

Lower Austria: Vöslau South of and adjoining Baden is the predominantly red wine area around the spa town of Bad Vöslau. These red wines are great favourites with the Austrians but I do not think they are much exported. Typically Vöslauer Rotwein is dark and pleasantly acidic, and made mainly from *Blau Portugieser* with some *Blau Burgunder* and *St Laurent*, grown on the typically 'poor' gravel red wine soil of the Steinfeld.

BURGENLAND

If it can be said in a general sort of way that the traditions of wine-making in Lower Austria are Germanic, those in the Burgenland are Hungarian. On the Austro-Hungarian frontier (which now is a typical fortified 'Iron Curtain' continuous frontier) these lands have suffered the grave disadvantages of disputed ownership over the centuries. They were Hungarian in the latter part of the Hapsburg monarchy, but most of them were ceded to Austria in 1921 under the terms of the Versailles Treaty. Wine production here is very ancient; there is said to be evidence that the Romans took over a thriving viticulture from the indigenous Celts. The climate and general environment, as will be seen later, make this particularly favourable country for wine-making.

The population now is mixed Austrian, Magyar and Croatian.

The dominant feature and centre of the most important viticulture is the large, shallow Neusiedlersee (also called Steppensee, or Fertö in Hungary, who still have a small share of it); this is a huge lake whose exact size varies continuously. It has disappeared completely and appeared again many times in the course of history and is at present 35 km wide. A belt of rushes about 1 km wide growing around the lake provides one of the richest bird sanctuaries in central Europe, and it is so shallow that it is possible to wade across it almost anywhere, the deepest part seldom exceeding 1 metre. This is also the hottest and dryest part of Austria under the influence of the 'Pannonian' climate system. The Austrians claim that the towns around the Neusiedlersee enjoy more sunny days than any other sun resort in this latitude in Europe.

It is clear, therefore, that the combination of this sort of weather with a large, shallow water surface with its capacity for heat storage and evaporation will create a microclimate ideal for viticulture.

The Burgenland at present makes nearly one third of Austria's wine production, but the Austrians are putting great efforts and much money into the development of wine-making here, so much more prominence will be given to Burgenland wines in the future. It is the main region in Austria for the making of red wine.

Burgenland: Rust This area covers the wine-making districts to the west of Neusiedlersee. The most famous wine town is Rust, 'the city of storks', formerly a Free City, and said to be the hottest and driest town in Austria. It has been noted for centuries for its Ruster Ausbruch, a rich, sweet wine of the type that reaches perfection in Tokaj. The Tokaji grape, *Furmint*, is grown here, with *Muskat-Ottonel* and the ausbruch (syrupy) wine is made from shrivelled *spätlese* grapes, but whether the sugar is concentrated by drying them in the sun or the action of *Botrytis cinerea* I do not know (I will give more space to this in the pages [84-93] devoted to Tokaj). None of the authorities claim the 'noble rot' so I assume the simpler method is used. Rust stands on a hill and the western side of the lake is bounded by the Leitha mountains. The soil here is limestone, and other grape varieties grown are *Wälschriesling, Neuburger, Weisser Bur-*

gunder, Traminer and, inevitably, *Grüner Veltliner*. Other noted wine villages on the western lakeside are Oggau, Mörbisch (famous for its Muskat wines), St Margarethen. Farther west, on the limestone slopes of the Leitha mountains are a string of wine towns, Eisenstadt (this is Esterházy country*), Gross- and Klein Höflein, St Georgen, Donnerkirchen, Purbach, Breitenbrunn, Widen, Jois and Neusiedl. There is an Austrian 'Turkish' joke about Purbach which tells of a Turk who drank too much of the local wine and hid up a chimney to sleep it off, whence he was smoked out. He was subsequently baptised and settled in the country, and the story is perpetuated on the labels of Purbach wines which show a turbaned Turk in an old chimney.

To the south-west of the Leitha mountain wine villages is the wine area around Pöttelsdorf and Mattersburg in the foothills of the Rosalien mountains, producing soft red wines from *Blaufrankisch (Gamay)* mainly, with some *Blauburgunder* and, a survival from the days of Hungarian occupation, *Kadarka*. Pöttelsdorfer Rotwein was the favourite tipple of Bismarck, which does not surprise me considering the paucity of drinkable red wine in his own country; and there is no doubt that this has for many hundreds of years been one of the principal red-wine-producing areas of Austria-Hungary.

Burgenland: Neusiedlersee The wine towns to the east of the lake are Weiden, Gols (the largest wine-growing community in Austria), Mönchhof and Halnturn to the north, making good full-bodied white wines from *Wälschriesling, Neuburger, Weisser Burgunder, Muskat-Ottonel* and *Traminer,* and benefiting, like the towns across the lake, from the specially favourable micro-climate of the lakeside areas.

Farther south, in the area formed by the shores of the lake and the Hungarian border, we have the area known as the Seewinkel (lake corner) with the towns of Podendorf, Illnitz and Apetlon, where the soil is drifting sand on which ungrafted vines will grow and flourish, because the Phylloxera louse will not

---

* This great Hungarian noble family has many claims to fame: to musicians for helping Franz Schubert when he most needed help and their liberal patronage of Joseph Haydn; to American wine lovers for their pioneer work in the establishment of the California vineyards. There are many other claims as well.

survive on it. Alas, although the vines will grow in the sand and the roots help to hold it together, there is not much in the way of extract to be taken from it and therefore the 'Sandwines', while plentiful enough, are never *Spitzenweinen* though perfectly adequate and useful *Tischweinen*. I believe most of the wine in this area comes from plantings of *Wälschriesling* and *Neuburger*, although *Rhineriesling* has been recently planted and is said to make good wine.

Burgenland: Eisenberg   South of the Neusiedlersee area and the Sopron region of Hungary (which is the only part of the Burgenland that she kept under the 1921 treaty) is a stretch of land from Lutzmannsberg in the north, through Rechnitz to Eisenberg, towards the border of the Styrian wine district; other names in this area are Neckenmarkler and Deutschkreutzer. In this part of Austria, and particularly around Eisenberg, are made pleasant soft red wines from *Blaufrankisch* and *Blau Portugieser*. The Eisenberg part of the Burgenland at present accounts for only one fifth of the Burgenland production.

Styria (Steiermark)

Part of ancient Illyria, Styria is quite separate from the other Austrian wine areas. It is rich, green, hilly pastoral country, bordering on Slovenia in Yugoslavia. Although there is variety in the soils, all the wine-growing is on hillsides, and there is evidence in the southern part of Styria that the Celts made wine there long before the coming of the Romans. Most of their production has, until recently at any rate, been consumed locally.

One of the problems in the wider marketing of Styrian wines has been the small quantities grown from a multiplicity of vine varieties, which may be the result of the local right exercised by Styrian growers to this day to sell their wines directly to consumers. However, more co-operatives are being organised, and without the services of such organisations, small growers all over Europe find it increasingly difficult to sell their wine profitably in the conditions of the European wine trade today. This also involves the 'rationalisation' of grape types, which is good for marketing if not carried too far – as it all too often is all over the world, for all kinds of fruit – and in the course of this process

AUSTRIA 45

excellent local types can be lost for ever. But that is too big a question to discuss in this book.

Styria: Southern Styria This area, of 900 hectares, is by far the biggest. The soil is heavy clay and the principal vines planted are *Wälschriesling,* with *Sauvignon, Weisser Burgunder* (called *Klevner* here), a *Muskat/Sylvaner* hybrid and a number of other vines in small quantities, such as the Hungarian *Yellow Muskateller, Gewürztraminer* and *Morillon,* most of them, I suppose, in danger of being grubbed up and planted with the more easily sold *Wälschriesling. Müller-Thurgau* was tried here, but the wine it made was not liked. At the southern extreme the towns of Glanz, Leutschach, Schlossberg, Ratsch, Ottenberg and Sutztal, with important centres at Spielfeld and Ehrenhausen should be noted. A little farther north and higher up in the hills is the area known as Sousal with the town of Kitzek (note that these are place-names with a Slovenian flavour) and Leibnitz the regional capital.

Styria: Klöch-East Styria A small, closed wine-producing area around the town of Klöch makes good wines from *Traminer, Walschriesling* and *Ruländer,* grown on old volcanic basalt soil – excellent for good wines. Some *Rhineriesling* and *Muskat/Sylvaner* are also planted here. Other names in the area to look out for are Radkersburg, Hartberg and Mureck on the river Mur, which forms the frontier with Slovenia.

Styria: West Styria As much north as west, this area covers the Styrian capital, Graz, and closed wine-making communities at Deutschlandberg, St Stefan o. St and Stainz. It is remarkable chiefly for a local *schilcherwein* – a kind of 'Siller' or rosé wine, made from a local vine, the *Blauer Wildbacher.* The colour of these wines ranges from rosé to ruby, and it has a piquant acidity. I do not think it has more than a local distribution, but in Styria it is very popular. A little white wine is made in West Styria from *Müller-Thurgau* and *Wälschriesling.*

It is apparent from what the Austrian Wine Institute tells me that the Styrian wine-growers are preparing for attacks on the export market, and if they make wines of good quality, there is a welcome for them.

Vienna

Although, as far as I know, none of the wines made in the Vienna wine district are exported (they can hardly have any to spare), no account of the wines of Austria would be complete without some words about one of her best-known and most popular tourist attractions – the *heurigen* which are taverns and wine gardens belonging, at any rate in theory, to wine-growers, where their own young wines are served, in an atmosphere of light music and general Viennese gaiety, green boughs being hung outside the little taverns as a sign that the young wines – the *heurige* – are ready. They are old in tradition and inevitably governed by Maria Theresa's wine laws. So popular are the *heurigen* that some of the proprietors must be hard pushed to produce enough wine from their own vineyards to meet the demand, and a new law (one that the Empress never had to imagine would be needed) makes it necessary for them to apply for special permits to sell wines from vineyards other than their own. The villages in the Vienna suburbs are Grinzing, Heiligenstadt and Nussberg, and in the Weinviertel, Perchtoldsdorf; there may be others but these are the best known, and the *heurige* wines are made from local vines – *Nussberger, Grinzinger* and *Sieveringer* as well as the native Austrian *Neuburger*.

Although the Viennese *heurigen* are best known and considerable tourist attractions, *heurigen* are found in most of the Austrian wine-making areas.

5
YUGOSLAVIA

A Socialist Federal Republic
Area: 255,800 square kilometres. Population: 19,280,000

A FEW almost random facts about this remarkable Federation of Republics will begin to give a picture of the Land of the Southern Slavs. It extends for 900 km from the Slovenian frontier with Austria to the Macedonian border with Greece, and 450 km from Dubrovnik on the Adriatic to the Hungarian/Romanian border: thus it is the biggest of the countries dealt with in this book, three times the size of Austria, and at least as great a proportion of its land surface is mountainous. It has four languages; Serbian, Croatian (these two are similar), Slovene and Macedonian; and two alphabets, Serbian and Macedonian being written in Cyrillic, Slovene and Croatian in Roman. It is populated by six major ethnic groups and at least seven minority groups.

The people of Slovenia and Croatia are predominantly Roman Catholic, those of Bosnia-Herzegovina predominantly Muslim, those of Serbia with Vojvodina predominantly Eastern Orthodox Christians, and the peoples of Montenegro, Kosmet and Macedonia are a mixture of Orthodox and Muslim; these, with substantial Protestant and Jewish minorities are all recognised by the State. The state consists of six Republics, each with its capital and government, with a Federal Government at Belgrade – something like the pattern of government in the United States. It has the most beautiful coastline in Europe, 600 km of it as the crow flies – ten times that length if one outlines every island, bay and creek. Above all it is an important wine-producing country.

The six Republics are, from north to south, as follows, and I give in each instance the percentage grown there of the total Yugoslavian wine production:

SLOVENIA, bordering Austria to the north, Hungary to the east and Italy to the west, with its capital at Ljubljana 9%

CROATIA, including Slavonia in the north, bordering Hungary, and Dalmatia from the Istrian Peninsular on the Adriatic to the border with Montenegro, with its capital at Zagreb 35%

SERBIA, including the autonomous provinces of Vojvodina in the north bordering on Hungary and Romania, and Kosmet in the south, bordering on Albania and Macedonia, with its capital at Belgrade, which is also the Federal capital 45%

BOSNIA-HERZEGOVINA, whose capital is Sarajevo 2%

MONTENEGRO, whose capital is Titograd negligible

MACEDONIA, bordered on the west by Albania, on the south by Greece, and on the east by Bulgaria. Its capital is at Skopje. 9%

(I make no apology for giving this detailed information as it is not as readily available as one would imagine. A very expensive internationally compiled atlas recently published had no single complete map of Yugoslavia.)

In 1970, 26,500 hectolitres of wine from Yugoslavia was imported into Great Britain, over 90% of it white wine.

Yugoslavia, like all the other countries of central and south-eastern Europe, has evidence of viticulture going back thousands of years, to Greek culture in Dalmatia and the Istrian Peninsular, and of course in Macedonia; and to Roman in the old Pannonian province, which covers eastern Slovenia and the Danubian Plain. But almost all her Balkan lands, virtually everything south of Slovenia and Slavonia, had been overrun by the Ottoman Turks by the end of the 15th century and they were not finally thrown out until the 1914-18 war. Naturally, more than four centuries of Muslem occupation has left indelible marks on the country; in fact, Sarajevo, the capital of Bosnia, is said to be the most Turkish city west of Istanbul. (It is interesting to note that modern Turkey has established a wine industry, but it is outside the scope of this book.)

The total area of wine cultivation is about 280,000 hectares and divided into six main regions, which will be later examined in some detail:

1. Slovenia
2. Slavonia
3. The Istrian Peninsular and Dalmatia
4. Herzegovina
5. Vojvodina
6. Serbia, Kosmet and Macedonia

It is remarkable that about 95% of the vineyards are still cultivated by peasant proprietors, although the marketing is in the hands of about ten State and co-operative agencies, making at any rate for a small measure of competition within the Federation. The opening up of markets – and not only in Europe – for the best of the central and south-eastern European wines, however, ensures that efforts are made to see that standards are established and observed and prices kept down. In fact, the standards in Yugoslavia are high, traditionally so in the northern parts and great efforts are being made to apply them in the Balkan lands where wine-making has a much more primitive background.

The Vines

Here there are language problems. In writing about Austria it seemed to me best to use the German names of well-known vines, including those from France, but from here on I shall give German names to Germanic vines and French to French vines; although there are many with names in one or other of the Yugoslavian languages. Where these can be translated and are familiar names, I will give the Yugoslavian name – or names – once only and then use the better-known name. As I wrote earlier, I have obtained many translations, but I am sure many of the Yugoslavian vines have more common names but have not been identified, and I shall be grateful if any readers who may know of some that I have not been able to identify will write to me care of my publishers so that any later editions may include this information.

First, then, let us list – mostly without comment, which will come later – the well-known European vines grown in Yugoslavia, starting with the white wine grapes and inevitably *Rhineriesling* (*Renski Riesling, Rajnski Rizling, Rajnai Grašvina*) and *Wälschriesling* (*Laški Riesling, Italijanski rizling, Grašvina, Grašica*). *Rhineriesling* is grown in Slovenia and Slavonia, probably introduced through Austria in the 19th century, *Wälschriesling* has been grown for a much longer time and I am sure it is better suited to the conditions of central Europe. It is grown in Slovenia, Slavonia and Vojvodina where I think it gives of its best, but more recently it has been introduced into Serbia, Kosmet and Macedonia where the results are, to me, altogether different. *Traminer* (*Traminac*) is grown in Slovenia, Slavonia and Vojvodina; *Sylvaner* (*Silvanec Zelini* = green) and also *Müller-Thurgau* (*Rizvanac Bijeli* = white) in Slovenia. *Sauvignon* is found in Slovenia, Slavonia, Vojvodina and Serbia; and *Sémillon* in Slovenia and Serbia. *Pinot Gris* (*Burgundac Sivi*, and often in Slovenia called by its Austrian name, *Ruländer*) grows in Slovenia and Slavonia, and a grape called Tokay in Slovenia may also be *Pinot Gris*. *Pinot Blanc* (*Beli Pinot*) is widely grown, being found in Slovenia and Slavonia, also in more recent plantings in the Serbia-Kosmet-Macedonia area in the south. *Chardonnay (Burgundac Beli)* is grown in Slovenia. I think it is true to say of these vines that, probably apart from those in Slovenia and part of Slavonia, most of them will have been planted in the post-war years as part of the efforts that are being made, and particularly since the political changes of 1953, to bring about a general improvement in the quality of the wines made in the more backward Yugoslavian viticultural areas.

Then there are a number of vines common to many of the central European countries – *Muskat-Ottonel* is grown in the southern Balkan states, and the *yellow Muskatteler* in Slovenia. *Furmint* (*Šipon, Moslavac Bijeli, Pošipon*) is found in Slovenia

YUGOSLAVIA

and Istria-Dalmatia and elsewhere, and so are the Austrian *Neuburger* and *Grüner Veltliner* (*Zleni Veltinac*). *Ezerjo* is grown in Vojvodina. The *Radgonska Ranina*, which grows in Slovenia, is the same as the Austrian *Bouviertraube précoce* (which means an early ripening grape).

This leaves a number of purely native vines of which the most commonly found is *Plavac*, both *Beli* (white) and *Zuti* (yellow) grown in Slovenia and Istria-Dalmatia. Others being very local are I think best mentioned when we deal with the areas in detail.

I will deal in the same way with the red wine vines. *Cabernet Franc* and *Cabernet Sauvignon* are grown in Slavonia, Istria-Dalmatia and Serbia-Kosmet-Macedonia; *Merlot* in Slovenia and Istria-Dalmatia. Of the Burgundian cépages, *Pinot Noir* (*Burgundac Črni* = black) is found in Istria-Dalmatia and Serbia-Kosmet-Macedonia, and *Gamay* (*Borgonja Črna* or *Frankinja Črna* or *Modra* = blue) in Slavonia and Serbia-Kosmet-Macedonia. As one would expect, Italian vines are grown in Slovenia and Istria-Dalmatia – *Barbera* and *Refosco* (*Terran Črni*). I suspect there are others but I have no translations reliable enough to commit to paper. Some Austrian vines are found – *Portugieser Rot* (*Kraljevina*) and *Blau Portugieser* (*Portugizac Črni* or *Portugalka*); *Rotgipfler* (*Želenac Slatki*); all in Slovenia and Slavonia. I wonder if I may safely guess *Šentlavrenka* or *Sentlovrenac* to be St Laurent? It grows in Slavonia and seems a safe assumption. However these guesses can be dangerous. Mr Bernhard Teltscher, in discussing this, told me of a Welshman who was convinced that the Russian General Timochenko was really a Welsh hero, Timothy Jenkins: on the other hand who is to say there may not be a grain of truth! The Grecian *Malvasia* (*Malvazija Istarska* = Istria) is vinified to make both red and white wines; *Kadarka* is extensively grown in the Balkan states – almost on its 'home ground' of Albania.

Apart from a number of purely local varieties, which we will note when we come to them in the individual areas, two native vines should be specially noted. *Mali* (= small) *Plavac* is used for red wines in the central European states (remember that a white Plavac is grown there for white wines); and *Prokupac Črni*, which is very extensively grown in the Balkan states.

As I wrote earlier, Yugoslavia's six main wine-producing areas are:

SLOVENIA (23,000 HECTARES OF VINEYARDS)

This is the most northerly of the Federated States and on the west adjoins the Friuli-Venezia Giulia area of Italy, including the enclave of Trieste, so that the Slovenian coastal area is of only a few kilometres. This is an 'intimate' sort of borderland – there is no geographical natural feature forming the frontier – and has in quite recent times been troublesome. Nevertheless, the western end of Slovenia is strongly influenced by the Adriatic Sea. To the north, Slovenia has a long frontier with Austria on the Alpine foothills of Carinthia and Styria of which, of course, in the old Hapsburg Empire it was part, and to the east, a short frontier with Hungary. It therefore has Italian, Austrian and to a lesser extent Hungarian influences, and is unquestionably the area producing the best wines. Because of the generally mountainous nature of the country, the wine-growing parts are in river valleys and the coastal plain. It is subdivided into four areas, the Drava banks, the Sava banks, the Primorsko-Kras area around Trieste, and Slovenian Istria, the last of these being a very small area.

Slovenia: the Drava banks To the east the mountainous country gives way to hills, river valleys and the Pannonian lowlands – and the country making the finest wines of Yugoslavia, lying on and between the valleys of the Mura and Drava rivers. It enjoys a climate combining Alpine moisture with Pannonian warmth. The subsoils in this region are of limestone and marl with rich alluvial deposits. But there is first a wholly white wine area north of the Mura river up to the Styrian and Hungarian frontiers, growing *Sylvaner*, *Wälschriesling* and *Müller-Thurgau* producing sound wines of no great distinction. Then south of the Mura and north of the Drava is the finest of the Slovenian – indeed of the Yugoslavian – wine areas, centred round the town of Maribor (where there is a Wine Institute) with Gornja Radgona to the north, Ljutomer-Ormož to the east and Ptny to the south. Again this is wholly white wine country, producing in the Ljutomer-Ormož area wines of great distinction from *Wälsch-*

and *Rhineriesling, Ruländer, Traminer, Sylvaner* and *Pinot Blanc*. These vineyards are the pride of Yugoslavia and in recent years have been quite lavishly equipped; nevertheless they have very old traditions of wine-making dating from pre-Roman times. This is a hilly area with a marl subsoil and argillaceous and sandy-argillaceous topsoils. The *Wälschriesling* from Ljutomer (Luttenberger in Hapsburg days) is surely too well known to need more comment. High on the Ljutomer-Ormož hills are the famous vineyards of Jeruzalem (named from its having been a favourite resting-place for Crusaders on their way to and from the Holy Wars) producing excellent wines from *Sauvignon, Ruländer,* and other 'noble' white wine grapes. Nicely balanced and certainly summing up in their aroma and flavour the best of Slovenian wine traditions. The rest of the Maribor area north of the Drava, a pleasant land of hills and river valleys, makes the whole gamut of white wine from light, dryish *Wälschriesling, Sylvaner* and *Müller-Thurgau* up to big, sweet *Muscats* and *Furmint*, and a local speciality made near the little Spa town of Kapela, the sweet Radgonska Ranina which has been given the fancy name of 'Tiger Milk' (I suppose in zoological rivalry with Hungary's 'Bull's Blood'). Also in Gornja Radgona is an old-established sparkling wine production, using the local *Riesling, White Pinot, Furmint, Müller-Thurgau,* and even the *Ranina (Bouvier).**

South of the Drava is another white wine area on the marl soils of south-facing slopes of the Halože hills. New vineyards are planted and old ones replanted here, with *Rhine-* and *Wälschriesling, Sylvaner, Traminer, White Pinot, Müller-Thurgau* and *Furmint*. This is good vine-growing country and the local 'Haložan' wines are popular. Other wine-growing regions in this area, many of them newly planted, are on the eastern and south-eastern slopes of the Pohorje and on the hills around Korjice.

Slovenia: the Sava banks This region is of gently wooded hilly country, producing white, rosé (Siller) and red wines. It is of secondary importance to the Drava valley area, but nevertheless makes good wines. We find here some purely native vines,

* This sparkling wine production was started by Clotar Bouvier the Elder; hence, I suppose, the name of the grape. This is one of many points needing further research.

notably *Plavac Beli* (white) and *Žuti* (yellow), sometimes grown here with *Wälschriesling*; Bizeljsko on the northern side of the Sava and not far from Zagreb the Croatian capital has more than local fame; and two red grapes *Žametovka and Žametna črnina*. A famous local wine – Cviček – is a 'Siller', a light ruby wine made from *Zametna črnina, Rot Portugieser* and the local version of *Gamay (Modra Frankinja)*. Cviček is light for this part of Europe and low in alcohol. It is matured in the cellars of the former Cistercian monastery at Kostajevica and the castle at Brežice. A darker, stronger red wine, Metliška črnina, is made on the southern slopes of the Gorjanci mountains from *Žametovka, Gamay* and *St Laurent*. They have a custom here of drinking the 'must' of *Blau Portugieser* as early as September, thereby outdoing *Beaujolais de l'année* by a good couple of months: a custom, I suggest, to be approached with some caution. The soil here is mainly marl as in the Drava country.

Slovenia: Primorsko-Kras The most westerly part of Slovenia bordering the Trieste 'corridor', and the little bit of Istria that just comes into Slovenia are all, of course, still Italianate in their traditions; hilly country and subject to the warm sea air from the Adriatic. From north to south there are four areas – Brda; Goriška and east of the Vipava valley; Kras (Karst) west of the Vipava valley; and Slovenian Istria. All this is ancient wine land, proud in tradition.

Brda is noted for the *Rebula* grape, growing on marl, making a dry full-bodied golden wine and I presume related to the *Ribolla* of Venezia Giulia. The Italian *'Tokay'* is also grown here, not the Hungarian *Furmint* but most likely the *Pinot Gris* or a near relative; and a little *Merlot*.

In the Goriška area they grow *Rebula*, a grape called *Pinela* which sounds Italian but may be purely local, *Zelen* which is the Austrian *Rotgipfler*, and *Wälschriesling*. A well-known local wine – Vipavac (known in the 16th century as 'Kindermacher' – baby maker) – is made from a blend of white wine grapes, mostly *Rebula, Pinela* and *Wälschriesling*. Some *Merlot* is grown here and makes a good red wine, probably worth maturing in bottle. The soil in these parts is partly limestone and part decayed marl. Mature old wine-growing country.

Kras, which means 'Karst', is characteristic high limestone

country, with sparse soil and rosemary and juniper growing wild; good country for red wines and famous since Roman times for its Kraski Teran, a wine, moderate in alcohol and high in extract. *Teran* or *Terran črni* is the Italian *Refosco*. *Barbera* is also grown here.

Slovenia: Slovenian Istria Hot coastal marl hills, this is Slovenia's only little bit of sea coast; growing olives as well as vines on terraces and making good rich white wines from *Malvasia* and *Muscat*, drier ones also from *Malvasia* and *White Pinot;* and deep red wines from *Refosco*, *Cabernet* and *Merlot*. It has a long history of wine-making and in the heyday of the Venetian Empire its rich desert Malvasia was much admired: it still is.

SLAVONIA (42,000 HECTARES OF VINEYARDS)

This is the northern vine-growing part of Croatia, lying between the valleys of the Drava and Sava rivers as far east as the Danube, and its northern boundary – the Drava – is the frontier with Hungary. In the considerable horse-trading that went on between Austria and Hungary under the Hapsburg Emperors, Slavonia – or Esclavonia as it was often called – was under the control of Hungary pretty well up to the First World War, and one of the most popular 'Hungarian' wines in Britain towards the end of the 19th century was Carlowitz (now Sremski Karlovci in Vojvodina), a red wine which it was claimed had remarkable curative properties. (In my Hungarian chapters I will enlarge a little on the subject of the British need for an excuse to drink and eat other than for simple enjoyment.) Little is heard of Carlowitz nowadays, these northern Slavonian lands mainly producing good white wines, the best of them on the Danube and Sava valleys near the border with Vojvodina in Serbia, around the towns of Slavonski Brod, Kutjevo, Erdut, Ilok, Vukover and Belji; and lesser white wines – strangely, as it seems to me – at the western end of Slavonia where it joins with Slovenia, north-east of Zagreb and not far from the fine Maribor area, areas about Vorazdin, Pljesevica, Vinica and Medjugorica. Both the *Rieslings* are grown, also *Pinot Blanc* and *Gris*, *Traminer* and *Sauvignon*, and Slavonian wines are said to 'approach' the quality of their Slovenian brethren, but are bigger, lower in acidity and alcoholically stronger. These qualities will make them less attractive in the northern European markets.

The Istrian Peninsular and Dalmatian Archipelago
(45,000 hectares)

This extraordinary strip of coastal country and islands extends for about 500 kilometres from the Istrian Peninsular to Dubrovnik and is all part of the Republic of Croatia – an ancient kingdom. Protected to the north and east by high mountains and bathed to the south and west by the balmy Adriatic, it is not surprising that it enjoys a rather special kind of climate – mild winters, early spring, rainy autumns and winters and hot Mediterranean summers. With the beauty of its coastline and mountain-backed landscape it has inevitably become internationally popular for holidays. It produces strong red and white wines, and we will deal with it as three separate areas.

Istria and the Kvarner This is most of the peninsular and the islands lying to the east of it. The traditional wine centre is Porec on the west coast, the site of an important agricultural college. The subsoil is limestone with a wide variety of deposits, and where the Kvarner region begins – and this includes the islands of Cres, Krk and some smaller ones – we approach Rijeka (which used to be called Fiume when these parts were Italian) and a more hilly 'karst' area. Sweet dessert wines are made from *Malvasia* and varieties of *Muscat*. It is also known for a bright ruby dessert wine made from a black Muscat. Red wines are made as well from *Refosco* (called *Teran*), *Gamay, Pinot Noir, Cabernet* and *Merlot*. The islands have a number of local vines whose names it would be of little value to list. This whole region produces wine, much of it sweet, delightful drunk there, though little of it is exported except some *Pinot, Cabernet* and *Merlot* which are big, deep pleasant wines. The Kvarner region has a tradition of sparkling wine production.

Dalmatia The narrow strip of coastal plain, mountain foothills and islands, facing south-west, punctuated by the towns of Zadar (Venetian Zara where Maraschino originated), Šibenik (once

A vineyard on the slopes of the Badacsony mountains on the north shore of Lake Balaton in Hungary. The basaltic rock structure can be clearly seen.

Typical low 'rock-hole' cellars deep in the Tokaj-Hegyalja hills in north-eastern Hungary, showing the characteristic 'gonci' casks.

The Lenz Moser 'high culture system', showing *above* how the vines are grown high and well-spaced; and *below* the wide distance between rows, allowing room for standard farm vehicles to be driven between them.

The illustrations give an idea of the modern 'wineries' in Slovenia, *above* being the surface buildings over the underground cellars at Ormoz; *below* a typical multi-storied storage tank installation.

the seat of Croatian kings), Split and Dubrovnik, and backed by the stark karst Dinaric Alps, a land of pines and olives as much as of vines, some growing on old, shallow terraces; settled by Greek vine-growers who came by sea up the Adriatic as early as the 6th century, these beautiful and eminently habitable lands have always been an important part of Mediterranean civilisation.

The northern part, from the Kvarner down to Šibenik, is predominantly a red wine area, using mainly local vines (many of them with strongly Italianate names), the principal ones being *Plavina* (or *Brajdica*) and *Babić*, making wines of those names, and a 'Siller' wine called Opolo, which is also found farther south. There are several local white wine grapes the most important to remember being *Maraština*, as that also makes very good wine down the coast.

From Šibenik down to Dubrovnik and beyond, including the islands, we have a more or less integrated wine-growing area, in spite of variations in soil, gradient and aspect of the vineyards, and even of climate. Almost all the vines are local types; the characteristic wine of the whole area is the red Plavac, made with the *Mali Plavac* grape. There are two special qualities of this wine, made of late-picked, sun-dried grapes, Dingač and Postup, both among the first Yugoslavian growths to be protected by law on much the same system as the French appellation laws. They are strong, dark red wines, full and sweetish in flavour, without being cloying. The rosé (Siller) wine of this area is Opol, which I mentioned earlier. These Opolo wines are made from a number of black grape varieties, the best being from *Plavac Mali*. Of white wines, the finest is Pošip, protected by law like Dingač and Postup. It is made from *Pošip* grapes, which I deduce to be *Furmint*, with *Maraština* and lesser amounts of other local varieties. It is a dryish wine of high extract.

Other similar white wines are *Maraština*, *Grk* and *Vagava* (made from grapes bearing those extraordinary names). The best Maraština is comparable with Pošip in quality and is legally protected – Maraština-Čara-Smokvica; but other wines from this grape and the *Grk* and *Vagava* wines tend to be too deep in flavour and with the slightly bitter finish found in white wines made in this sort of climate to suit our taste, pleasant as they are when drunk in Dalmatia with the local food. There is a typical Dalmatian dessert wine called Prošek made from *Maraština, Vagava, Grk* and *Pošip,* the strength and concentration of which are claimed to be 'natural', i.e. the must is not fortified.

The Imotski Region   The Dalmatian hinterland, centred round the town of Imotsko, is a link between the Mediterranean climate and the conditions of the coastal area, and the 'continental' conditions of Herzegovina in Bosnia. Red and white wines of good quality but no great distinction are made from local vines, the names of which we need not add to an already complicated list.

Herzegovina

This, the only serious wine-producing part of Moslem Bosnia, makes only 2 per cent of Yugoslavia's wines in an area of about 5,000 hectares, but this includes what some authorities consider the greatest of Yugoslavian white wines – Mostarska Žilavka. The centre of the wine trade is Mostar, the provincial capital, a charming town, and the vineyards are on the slopes of the Neretva valley. 80% of the production is of white wines, mostly from the excellent regional vine, *Žilavka* which on the limestone subsoils produces surprisingly light, distinguished wine, without the characteristic flavours one usually finds – and dislikes – in white wines grown at this latitude. The red wine is made from another purely native vine, *Blatina*; undistinguished, and usually blended with *Kadarka, Plavka* and other local types.

Vojvodina (25,000 hectares of vineyards)

This is an autonomous province of Serbia. Here we go north again back into the Pannonian plain, east of Slavonia and bordering on Hungary and Romania; and one of Yugoslavia's most important agricultural areas. Table as well as wine grapes are grown here. There are three districts – Fruška Gora, the Subotiča sand plains and the Banat.

Fruška Gora   A gentle, wooded mountain on the southern bank of the Danube, which runs east-west here just before turning north into Hungary; lime and loess subsoils and the 'Pannonian' climate, which we have met before. Clearly the Yugoslavians are developing here intensively with large plantations of vines and modern vinification units; and, I am afraid, rationalisation of vine sorts, as they have discovered that our old friend *Wälschriesling* does very well here. They also grow *Sémillon* and *Sauvignon, Traminer, White Pinot* and *Sylvaner*. The best vineyard areas are at Sremski Karlovci (the Carlowitz of Hapsburg days), Erdovic and Vrdnik. I do not know, rightly popular as it is, whether there may not tend to be over-production of *Wälschriesling*. However, they are also extending their plantings of *White Pinot* and *Sylvaner* and it will be interesting to see how they develop. Sound as they are, the wines made here do not reach the quality of the Maribor production. Sremski Karlovci was once a considerable red wine area and the *Bouvier* was extensively grown. I have not tasted the wine of this grape, but it is said to be 'very heavy and strong, lacking in harmony and acidity but very suitable for improving low-quality wines'. The local wine is Plemenka, made from grapes, red and white, of that name, with *Bouvier* and other local varieties. The tendency is to go over to white wines and to replant the red wine vineyards with the Burgundian vines. *Prokupac*, an important Balkan vine, was grown here but is being replaced. There is a red aromatic wine, a kind of Vermouth, made at Sremski Karlovci since the 18th century, called Bermet, based, at any rate nowadays, on *Gamay* and *Pinot Noir* flavoured with wormwood, sugar and other flavours and fortified: also a sparkling wine, Fruškogorski biser.

Subotička Peščara Reclaimed sand plains (this is an extension of the Hungarian Alföld) between the Danube and Tisza rivers, growing, until recently, poor quality local vines. A policy of improved plantings is being applied here and such varieties as *Grüner Veltliner, Wälschriesling, Ezerjo* and *Muskat Ottonel* are growing, together with a good local variety, *Kevedinka*. As in Hungary and parts of the Burgenland in Austria, vines growing on sand are prolific enough and produce a useful neutral sort of wine, but rarely, to my knowledge, of any great quality. For red wines *Kadarka* and *Pinot Noir* are grown, again making what are described as 'wines suitable for blending', and much in demand in West Germany.

The Banat Most of the Banat is now in Romania. The Yugoslavian part consists of land east of the Tisza and north of the Danube. Part of it – the Banatska Peščara – is sand land similar to that of Subotička and the Hungarian Plain, but unsuitable for cultivation owing to the very deep water table. Nevertheless the Banat accounts for two thirds of the vineyard area of Vojvodina, but as table grapes are grown here I do not know how much of this is wine-producing. However, in spite of climatic disadvantages peculiar to the area, there is substantial wine production, including vineyards at Vršac which were planted there by the Romans. Remember, too, that the Banat was occupied by the Turks for two hundred years or so. Vršac is the centre of wine production here, and has an Oenological Centre and College. About 300,000 hectolitres are made annually, of which one third is of high quality. This is primarily a white wine district and has its own version of *Riesling – Banatski Rizling-Kreaca –* which is frost-resistant, apparently an important quality here. Other than this, the same kinds of vines are planted as in the Fruška Gora. A little red wine is made, mainly from *Gamay, Merlot, Pinot Noir* and *Prokupac*.

To sum up, I think it is fair to say that Vojvodina is in process of finding its feet in modern international conditions. It clearly does not produce wines of the highest quality, but is geared to make quantities of good ordinary wine, for which there is an ever-increasing world demand.

SERBIA, KOSMET AND MACEDONIA (150,000 HECTARES)

This, Yugoslavia's eastern and southern wine-growing region, produces more than half of her wine and most of her table grapes. It is nearly all mountainous and the vineyards are, as one would expect, in river valleys. They stretch from the eastern end of the Serbian province of Vojvodina and the south Banat on the Romania frontier, down to the frontiers with Greece and Albania; from north to south well over 400 kilometres. This is Balkan wine made mostly from Balkan native grape varieties, and much less infiltrated by western European vines and practices than most of the other areas of Yugoslavia. Let us look at these areas.

Serbia From the Danube valley at Belgrade there are stretches of vine-growing country in the valley of the Morava river almost up to its source; and another on the Danube valley from its confluence with the Timok and into the big bend that is the Romanian frontier. I shall always have a sentimental fondness for Serbian wine because, at the end of the war, starved for years of any sort of decent wine, we were lucky enough to come across in north Germany a cache of 'Servian Rotwein', spoils of war, good honest stuff that had some age in bottle and washed down the rations very pleasantly for some months – in fact until I was moved to another and utterly wine-less place.

Serbia is the home of two good indigenous vines – *Smederevka*, a white grape which is grown both for wine-making and as a table grape. It is frequently blended nowadays with *Wälschriesling*, and at its best makes a very acceptable wine. The other is *Prokupac*, popular with vine-growers because of its disease-resistance, rich yields and resistance to frosts. I expect my 'Rotwein' was made from it. I have tasted many wines made from *Prokupac*: at its best, I think, as a rosé (Ružica), and at its worst, I must say, it can be very rough and ordinary. Vinified right out on its skins, it produces a very deep-coloured wine and I am sure would be improved with great care and time spent in vinification and maturing, but here we are back at the old problem of economics – is *Prokupac* worth more time and expense in the making? The Serbian wine-makers are more and more blending *Prokupac* with other wines such as *Gamay*, with happy results.

The soils vary considerably in this area; essentially loess subsoils in the Danube and lime farther south on the Morava valley, with a considerable variety of surface soils.

The Serbian winelands start in the immediate outskirts of Belgrade, around Smederevo, in lands where the Romans made wine in the 1st-3rd centuries A.D. (The grape *Smederevka* takes its name from the town.) It is one of the most important fruit-growing areas in the whole of Yugoslavia and grows its namesake as much as a table grape as for wine-making. 80 per cent of the wine made in this area is white, mostly *Smederevka* and, increasingly, *Wälschriesling*, which is said to make excellent wine here as also does *Traminer*: acceptable, dryish white wines.

The farther south one goes, the more the growing of white wine vines gives place to red, mostly *Prokupac* with lesser quantities of another local vine – *Plovdina*. A high proportion of the *Prokupac* is vinified to produce the Siller wine (just too ruby to called rosé) Ružica. One of the best, Jovačka Ružica, is claimed to have a bouquet 'reminiscent of wild roses' – and very nice too. Again it is necessary to kill the legend, which dies hard, that rosé wines are as light in alcohol as they are in colour. Nowhere is this less true than in these Serbian Ružica wines which are often as strong as 13% or more G.L.

The Župa district, centred on Aleksandrovac just below Kruševac, with vineyards on mountain slopes, is claimed to be the real home of *Prokupac* and, in good years, to produce wines from it that 'can be classified as fine'. A little white wine is made as far south as this from *Wälschriesling, Žilavka, Furmint* and *Sémillon*, but it is high in alcohol and low in acid, not the sort of white wine that the English like. In the far south of Serbia proper in a predominantly *Prokupac-Plovdina* area they make a wine called Grom (which means thunder), with an alcohol content of 14% G.L., dark colour and low acidity: just a warning. But to counteract this there is a pleasant white wine made from *Prokupac* and *Plovdina* called Vlasotinačka Plemenka 'much appreciated by people who suffer from hyper-acidity'.

Finally, there is the small area near the Romanian frontier on the Danube – the Timok area – growing *Prokupac, Plovdina, Začinka* (another local type) and *Smederevka* for white wines, none of them I think making wines of any special distinction; but they also make a pink-juice rosé (i.e. one that does not take its colour from lying on the skins) from *Bagrina* which is a vine grown in neighbouring Romania and may have originated in Turkey. The Germans call it *Gewürztraube* which gives a clue to its flavour: and a wine from *Muskat-Hamburg* which may be the Black Hamburgh which grows so well in my garden in Kent.

Kosmet An autonomous province of Serbia. The vineyards grow on the foothills of lofty mountains and many of them were first planted there by the ancient Greeks, on a great variety of soils and subsoils. This region adjoins Albania, lies roughly between the towns of Peć to the north and Prizren. It consists mainly of the Kosovo Pilje (= field; in German *Amselfelder* and you will see why later). This was the scene of a famous battle with the Turks six hundred years ago. After the destruction of the vines here by Phylloxera at the turn of the century many of the vineyards were not replanted until as recently as ten years ago and this probably accounts for the presence here of many western European vines e.g. *Gamay, Pinot Noir, Cabernet Franc* (most of the wine made here is red). The best of the small amount of white wine grown here is made from *Žilavka* and *Wälschriesling*. Wine made in this district from *Pinot Noir* is the most popular Yugoslavian wine in West Germany where it is sold as *Amselfelder Spätburgunder*.

Macedonia Most of this Republic is mountainous, but she has important grape production along the valley of the Vardar river (and this is mostly of table grapes of which Macedonia makes two thirds of Yugoslavia's production); and lesser areas around the great mountain lakes in the extreme south-west at the Albanian-Greek frontiers, and on the Osogovska hills to the east, bordering on Bulgaria. The vineyards are high, up to 1000 metres. They grow the indigenous types – *Prokupac, Plovdina, Stanušina*, the Montenegrin *Vramac* for red wines, the main production; and for the few white wines the Serbian *Smederevka* and Herzegovinan *Žilavka* and, inevitably, *Wälschriesling*. I have tasted Macedonian wines on many occasions and cannot escape the conclusion that this is not a true wine-growing area – I grade them from very rough to ordinary. On the other hand, I have for many years believed that Macedonia grows the best tobacco in the world.

Montenegro A little wine is made on the Adriatic coastal strip and around Lake Skadar in this otherwise wild mountainous country, not significant quantities and probably never seen outside Montenegro. The areas have two grapes of their own, *Vramac* which makes wine of an intensely deep colour, and *Kratošiza* with its greater acidity. Between them they are said to make a wine 'of pleasant flavour and characteristic aroma'. I am sure it tastes marvellous out there.

6
HUNGARY
(*Magyarország*)

A Socialist Republic
Area: *93,000 square kilometres*. Population: *10,250,000*

THE finest wines of central and south-eastern Europe are made in the ancient kingdom of Hungary: and some of the finest wines of Hungary are in their styles the greatest in the world, and have been so recognised for centuries. Let me quote again from Cyrus Redding. In the introduction to his *A History and Description of Modern Wines* published in London in 1833 he writes:

The French wines are the best and purest, and not these alone, but the German and Hungarian wines are, besides their purely vinous qualities, among the most delicate and perfect in character. I have, therefore, been governed by truth and not by predilection, in making them the superior in every possible sense, and I do not think I am wrong.

Again, in writing specifically of Hungarian wines:

The wines of Hungary have long enjoyed a well-merited fame, and . . . they rank so high in the highest class of the products of the vintage, that they have borne the name of Hungarian wine far beyond where it has ever been tasted or seen.

The Hungarian people – the Magyars – are unique in this part of Europe. They are not Slavs nor are they Teutons or Latins, and that their extraordinary qualities of intelligence and tenacity should have survived intact through a history so violent, even by Balkan standards, proves, I think, that these Magyar qualities may well be her greatest asset: for the country has no great natural resources and she has always had to struggle to survive and prosper, in the best sense, by her wits. And in this she has, on the whole, triumphantly succeeded. Even in the present century she has lived through dramatic changes that would have finished many lesser peoples: none of my readers will have forgotten the tragic events of 1956 and all that led up to them. Once more she had to start again as she has had to so often before, and Hungary now appears to have reached a state of balance, even of quiet prosperity and – dare I say? – of slowly increasing liberalisation in her whole social and economic structure.

I am sure I do not need to remind my readers of the great contribution the Magyars have made over the centuries to the arts, and particularly to music, with great composers from Liszt to Bartok and Kodály, and pianists and string players of the highest eminence in a never-ending stream: and nowadays she appears to supply the rest of Europe with economists! Her religious traditions are about two-third Catholic and the rest Calvinist.

Above all, from our immediate point of view, she has never lost her ability to preserve and exploit the wonderful assets she possesses as a maker of wine.

I must keep within bounds references to a long and complex history and only refer to the parts of it which are relevant in discussing the various wines.

Unlike all her neighbours, Hungary has no high mountain ranges; two-thirds of the land surface is less than 200 m above sea level, with one peak, Mount Kékes of 1055 m in the Mátra hills as the highest point. The country falls naturally into four regions, determined by her principal geographical features, the two great rivers, Danube and Tisza; the Great Plain (Alföld) covering nearly half the country to the east up to the frontier with Romania, and with main centres at Debrecen in the north and Szeged in the south; the Small Plain (Kisalföld) in the north-western corner, centred on the town of Györ; Transdanubia to the west, between the Danube and the Drava, which forms the boundary with Slovenia and Slavonia, with the great lake Balaton in the middle and Pécs as the main town; and the

E

Northern Massif, extending east from the great bend of the Danube north of Budapest, consisting of the Carpathian foothills and most of the Slovakian frontier, the main town being Miskolc, the most important industrial city after Budapest. Few of us are familiar with Hungarian geography and I think it will help if I refer to these four regions in identifying the positions of the wine districts as we deal with them.

The Hungarian climate is temperate, free from the extreme influences that characterise the climates of many of her neighbours for good or ill, and without great regional variations. It is fairly predictable and certainly enjoys more sunshine than western European countries in the same latitude.

Hungary has about 200,000 hectares of vineyards which, in relation to her overall area, and compared with her Yugoslavian and Romanian neighbours, is a very high proportion of her total agricultural land. Only about 15% of her grape harvest is of table grapes and her average wine production is about 5 million hectolitres.

Let me digress a little here about these 'league tables' of national wine production and whatever merit they may have to express my distrust of the usefulness of a system that does not distinguish quality. For example, the French figures equate for statistical purposes the greatest products of the Médoc and the Côte d'Or with the rough Midi wines, on the distillate of which I remember in the immediate post-war years, when petrol was still scarce, the French used to run their cars and lorries. Perhaps one day this distinction will be universally applied; meanwhile it is worth keeping in mind, when considering and comparing these figures: I mention it here because clearly the Hungarian production will include an appreciably greater proportion of wine of high quality than those of her neighbours.

On the basis of a detailed survey and registration of all the vineyards of Hungary completed in 1956, the country was divided into fourteen wine districts. In order to simplify, however, I group some together where this can logically be justified.

1. Tokaj-Hegyalja (the northern massif)   6,225 hectares

2. Badacsony
   Balatonfüred-Csopak   (Transdanubia)   6,450 hectares
   Balaton

These three districts cover all the vineyards
growing on the northern side of Lake Balaton.

3. BÁRSONYOS-CSÁSZÁR
   MÓR } (Transdanubia) 1,800 hectares

4. EGER (the northern massif) 3,150 hectares

5. MÁTRAVIDÉK (the northern massif) 12,300 hectares
   The region of the southern foothills of
   the Mátra Mountains.

6. MECSEK
   VILLÁNY-SIKLÓS
   SZEKSZÁRD } (Transdanubia) 4,280 hectares
   These three districts form a group to
   the south of Transdanubia.

7. SOMLÓ (Transdanubia) 435 hectares
   An isolated site to the west of
   Transdanubia.

8. SOPRON (The Small Plain) 1,300 hectares
   This is the only part of the Burgenland
   left to Hungary.

9. THE GREAT PLAIN 95,000 hectares
   Vineyards spread all over the area between
   the Danube and Tisza, from the outskirts of
   Budapest right down to the frontier with
   Vojvodina.

Those mathematicians who have added up the areas set out above and found the total short of the 200,000 hectares that I mentioned earlier will like to know that there are 'unregistered' wine and grape districts at Dunántuli in Transdanubia, Felföldi in the northern massif and a place called Nyirség that I cannot find on any map, all of which I am told 'are of no significance from the point of view of quality production'.

Part of the wine-making is in the hands of peasant proprietors, either working individually or as members of cooperatives, and partly on huge State Farms. I do not know exactly the proportion of each but I do know that the majority if not all the growths on which the fame of Hungarian wine rests are still made by peasant proprietors and that, as in all modern wine-producing countries, their methods right through the whole process from grafting and planting the vines to vinification and the maturing of the wine are constantly reviewed and improved in the light of modern knowledge of this complicated subject. The Hungarian Viticultural and Oenological Research Institutes have long been world-famous.

The annual consumption of wine per head in Hungary averages about 26 litres which is roughly in line with the other countries in this part of Europe. She has a world-wide export trade, which of course is not new, as it is with most of her neighbours, but has waxed and waned with her political and economical fortunes; and in the period between the wars probably reached its lowest ebb. It is now thriving and no other country in Europe, in my view, has the potential that Hungary has to meet the growing demands for wines of high quality at reasonable prices. In 1970 Hungary exported over 9,500 hectolitres to the United Kingdom.

Of the nine wine areas set out above, I will devote the special chapter to the Tokaj-Hegyalja wines that they clearly deserve, but before dealing in detail with the others, I will make our customary examination of the vines used in this most fascinating of wine countries.

The Vines

In Hungary we find more 'native' vines and fewer of the western European varieties than in any other of the countries studied in this book. On the other hand, many of the vines widely grown in Hungary are found in other parts of central Europe and the Balkans. Again there are language problems, but I have had access to much detailed information and many excellent translations and I think it unlikely that there are any ambiguities and others of the problems that are bound to appear in work of this kind. The Hungarians are rightly very proud of the best of their native varieties.

As with the other countries, let us first deal with the 'universal' varieties beginning with the white wine vines. Not surprisingly *Wälschriesling* (*Olaszrizling*) is very extensively grown and, I think, produces its best wine in Hungary. It is found in all parts

HUNGARY

of the country except the specialist areas such as Tokaj (where extraneous vines are strictly forbidden) and Mór, and of course the purely red wine areas of Eger and Villány-Siklós. The *Rhineriesling* (*Rajnairizling*), as far as I can discover, is only planted in a very small way in the Somló area. *Sylvaner* (*Zöldszilváni, Szilváni*) is grown in parts of the Balaton area and is a recent experiment there. I have not tasted the wine it produces and the Hungarians make little of it. *Traminer* (*Piros = red Tramini*) is grown in the Somló and Sopron areas, and this is probably because they are both areas near the present frontier with Austria. The Hungarian *Szürkebarát* (which means Grey Friar) is a type of *Pinot Gris* and is grown only in the Badacsony vineyard on Lake Balaton where it makes a wine of very high quality. *Pinot Blanc* (*Fehér*=white *burgundi*) is found in the Mecsek area in Transdanubia. The Austrian *Veltliner* is grown a little in the Sopron area, again not surprisingly; and *Muskats* – *Sárgamuskotály* (*yellow Muskat*) in the Tokay area and *Ottonel* (*Ottonelmuskotály*) in the Great Plain. *Chasselas* is grown to produce table grapes.

Then there are some vines common to other central European and Balkan countries. *Ezerjó* (a Hungarian word meaning 'a thousand boons' but I believe the vine came originally from India) is grown widely in the Great Plain and a little in the Balaton area, but makes a wine of real quality in the Mór district. *Leányka* (another Magyar word meaning 'young girl'; the Hungarian grape names always mean something – one could almost call them nicknames) is the same as the Romanian *Feteasca alba*. It is found on the Great Plain and in parts of the large Mátravidék area where it makes excellent wines of great charm. Finally of course the noble *Furmint,* the principal type grown to make Tokaji and also found in parts of the Balaton, Mecsek and Somló areas, everywhere making wines of high quality and distinction. *Kovidinka,* a vine grown on the Great Plain is probably the same as the Vojvodinan *Kevedinka*: *Dinka* is a type of vine found in many parts of the Balkans and as far as I know it has no claims to nobility.

The purely Hungarian white wine vines found, to the best of my knowledge only in that country, must begin with *Hárslevelü* (which means 'Lime' and refers to its characteristic leaf shape) makes with *Furmint* and a little *yellow Muskat* the great wines of Tokaj. It is also grown in other parts of the northern massif. *Mézesfehér* (mézes means honey and fehér, white) grows on the Great Plain, Balaton and the Mátravidek area and its name gives a fair description of the kind of wine it produces: unfashionable over here, but what a pity! *Kéknyelü* (Kék means blue and the name means 'blue stalk' describing a characteristic of the vine) is peculiar to the Badacsony area and makes an excellent, deep golden wine. Also in this area a vine called *Budai* is grown but I have never tasted the wine it makes. Its name obviously comes from its place of origin, but the vineyards that used once to grow on land that is now part of the capital no longer exist; Budapest has no 'heurigen'. A little of a vine called *Juhfark* (meaning 'lamb's tail') is grown in the Somló area but I doubt if its wine is ever vinified separately and I mention it for its whimsical name. Two other vines producing uninteresting, neutral sort of wine, useful for making *sekt* in Germany and that kind of thing and grown only on the Great Plain are *Sarfehér* and *Szlankamenka,* but as the whole tendency to improve the quality of vines grown has gone far in Hungary they may well be in the process of being replaced by vines of better quality.

That accounts for the important white wine vines which in Hungary are the most numerous, as 70 per cent of her production is of white wines; but the red wines are important and some of them of excellent quality.

The best red wines of Hungary are made from *Pinot Noir* (*Nágyburgundi*) particularly in the Villány-Siklós district; *Gamay* (*Kékfrankos*) in the Sopron area only; and the Balkan *Kadarka,* which makes wines of quality in Hungary, both in the Siller style and fully vinified. *Kadarka* is very extensively grown on the Great Plain where the conditions suit it admirably; in the Mátravidek area in the northern massif; and in Eger, where it is an ingredient of the well-known 'Bull's Blood'. The Bordeaux cépages, *Médoc Noir (Merlot), Cabernet Franc* and *Cabernet-Sauvignon* are also grown in the Eger district and nowhere else that I can discover; and the Austrian *Blau Portugieser* is grown in Villány-Siklós. There is thus, excluding the Balkan *Kadarka,* no 'native' Hungarian red wine grape, although I think that there is no doubt that *Kadarka* has found in Hungary the conditions that suit it best and it makes some excellent wine there.

HUNGARY

Before I go on to more detailed descriptions of the individual wine districts, I will digress again to touch on a subject I mentioned earlier, and that is the extraordinary British characteristic that it is somehow sinful to enjoy what we eat and drink (though there are now signs that we are fast growing out of it; we eat bad food for quite different reasons now). In fact such Puritanism carried to its extreme even held that enjoyable food and drink were likely to be bad for you.

I remember that my paternal grandmother, a most devout old lady, held this belief very strongly and put it into practice in her cooking, producing meals which I have no doubt were nourishing – they were certainly claimed to be wholesome – but which as a young lad I used to dread having to eat: but I was lucky that my maternal grandmother inherited and, mercifully, passed on to my mother a tradition of English country cooking at its best. Maybe she was less devout – or could it have been that the Puritan traditions were stronger or lingered on longer in the towns than in the country? However, my point is that up to the last war – and in remote pockets still for all I know – all wine merchants listed 'Invalid' Port, 'Tonic' Australian Burgundy and a whole gamut of wines of one sort and another whose sole *raison d'être* was their alleged tonic or curative properties; and brandy of course was considered strictly a medicine. I mention all this here because it illustrates an example of Hungarians using their wits in the last century. Up to 1865 or thereabouts, foreign wine, with the exception of Port, was subject to prohibitory duty, and had been for about two centuries. W. E. Gladstone, then Chancellor of the Exchequer, to his eternal credit slashed this duty and opened the British market to a flood of foreign table wine. The Hungarian wine merchants of that time attacked the market strongly and successfully through the Doctors, by sending them generous samples of Hungarian wines, with eulogies of their marvellous medicinal qualities, to the consternation of the English wine trade, one member of which wrote in 1877:

The popularity for a while was due to the persevering energy of some of its active vendors, who by a certain specious liberality sent cases of an assortment of Hungarian wines to the medical profession throughout the kingdom. These presents were accompanied with an analysis of the hygienic properties of the wine, and the recipients were solicited to recommend the wine to their patients as being that of all others most beneficial for invalids.*

The writer goes on to deplore the advertising methods adopted, including a whole column in the London *Times* at the enormous cost of £30!

Hungarian wines more than any others have for centuries had the most extraordinary magical powers attributed to them, as we shall see when we deal with them in detail. The properties of Tokaj Essenz as an aphrodisiac are legendary, but more than this, it had – and still has as I am assured – the reputation for sustaining, even renewing life itself: and the wine of Somló had philoprogenitive powers which were recognised all over Europe, not least by our own Queen Victoria! So let us look more closely at these remarkable wines as they exist today.

Tokaj-Hegyalja

This needs a chapter to itself, which follows.

Badacsony – Balatonfüred-Csopak – Balaton

These three of the fourteen officially designated wine districts are all on the north side of Lake Balaton, 'The Hungarian Sea', partly on slopes, facing south-east and it will therefore be convenient to deal with them together. The first two districts produce wines which are justly designated as being of outstanding quality, the third covers the rest of the vineyards growing on the northern lakeside and making wines of high quality.

The lie of the land in this beautiful part of Hungary – Transdanubia, a large part of the Roman Province of Pannonia – is in a north-east to south-west direction, with the rolling wooded Bakany Hills, starting at the bend of the Danube north of Budapest extending for nearly 200 kilometres, and Lake Balaton below the southernmost end of them. The long, fairly narrow fresh-water lake has a shore line of nearly 300 km and, with the gentle hills behind it, makes a landscape which a Magyar

---

*Charles Tovey: *Wines and the Wine Countries,* London 1877.

writer describes as of 'soothing charm producing poetry'. There is none of the menacing majesty of high mountain scenery in Hungary.

Balaton has a microclimate similar to that of the Neusiedlersee in the Burgenland, with the perfect aspect of the vineyards and the reflections and heat-absorbing properties of the large water surface, combined with the Pannonian climate making it an ideal setting for vineyards. Viticulture here can be traced back over at least 2000 years and it was a favourite wine area of the Romans, who transported wine from the Badacsony vineyards to the Emperors in Rome. The foundations of the road on which it was transported still exist and the whole area is rich in remains of the Roman civilisation here, some of them with representations of viticultural and vintage scenes.

The Badacsony district consists of volcanic hills, the best known being Mount Badacsony (438 m), St George (Szentgyörgyhegy) (414 m) and the lesser Szigliget. Their heat-absorbing basaltic subsoils with topsoils of loess, sand and clay combined with their aspect and the climate with the Balaton microclimate make this a perfect site for wine-making. The Roman cultivation was for centuries continued and improved by monastic orders, with their unerring nose for good wine-producing sites in which to establish themselves. Many of the vineyards – 1850 hectares of them – are on terraced sites on the hillsides and I believe that it is here that the *Wälschriesling* produces its superb best. It was extensively planted here after the Phylloxera devastation and makes wine, like all those of this area, rich in extract. But this is the home of *Kéknyelü*, which makes a delightful green-golden wine with a distinctive bouquet and balanced flavour. *Kéknyelü* is a vine of low yield, and must always be relatively expensive. The other widely grown vines here are *Pinot Gris* (*Szürkebarát*), which makes a rich, almost dessert wine and the native *Zöld*=green *Budai*. There is an important viticultural institute devoted largely to the study of this ancient area and the Balaton district generally, and to the preservation and improvement of the vines that flourish here. At one time as many as seventeen varieties were cultivated in the Badacsony district, but they are now restricted to those that do best – those already mentioned being the most successful, with some *Furmint* and the *yellow Muskat*.

The Balatonfüred-Csopak district of 1400 hectares at one time formed part of the Badacsony district, with as ancient a history going back to pre-Roman times, but it is now treated separately, largely becaue of the different geological structure and wine characteristics. The vineyards are again on gentle hillsides on a subsoil of crystalline slate covered with red sandstone and limestone with a topsoil of Pannonian sand. The red soil here is rich in iron.

(The presence of sand of various depths as part of the soil structure of many parts of ancient Pannonia, not only in Hungary but also in Austria, Vojvodina and Romania, is due to the action of the so-called Pannonian Sea which covered this part of Europe in the course of the evolution of its present shape hundreds of thousands of years ago.)

This part of Balaton enjoys a particularly warm, sunny climate which gives it the nickname of 'The Hungarian Riviera' and makes wines, softer than those of Badacsony, but of great elegance, sometimes even of delicacy, from *Wälschriesling, Furmint* and *Sylvaner*. It is interesting to taste the difference in the quality of *Furmint* grown here and at Badacsony with the quite different wine it makes in Tokaj. The wines of this district are of very good quality and with high extract.

The vineyards on the north of Lake Balaton which are not included in the foregoing two quality districts are extensive – 3,200 hectares – and make good quality wines from *Wälschriesling, Mézesfehér, Ezerjó* and, more recently, *Sylvaner*. They are pleasant and very much of the popular style, lighter and softer than those of Badacsony and Füred. There is great variety of soils, including those already listed in the high quality area with some areas of red trachyte and thick clay. Wine has been made all along these shores for at least a couple of thousand years and it is clearly one of Nature's great vineyards.

Bársonyos-Császár, Mór

By Hungarian standards much of this is comparatively new vine-growing country. It is in the Bakany hill country between Budapest and the northern part of Lake Balaton. The Bársonyos-Császár district of 700 hectares was in fact only established in 1959 but is on part of an older district – Neszmély – which practically went out of cultivation after the Phylloxera devastation. The vineyard areas are of Pannonian sand and clay on marl and loess. Parts of the Bársonyos area together with the more important centre of Mór (of which Császár was until recently a part) were first settled and planted with vines in the mid-18th century by Bavarian wine growers on cleared woodlands. I know little about the Bársonyos-Császár district which clearly the Hungarians are still busy developing, and they have not told me what vines they are planting there, but the Mór district, which consists of the village of Mór and five other hill villages amounting to about 1100 hectares, has several matters of interest to us. In the first place the sandy soil there, with a high quartz and mica content on dolomite rocks, is almost immune from the Phylloxera aphid. Without going into the sordid details of its breeding and life cycle, it is a fact that the aphid cannot breed in the physical environment of sand, and thus Mór is one of the few places that escaped the worst ravages of Phylloxera and the vines are still grown there on the original Magyar stock: and the vine that is grown practically exclusively there is *Ezerjó* – 'a thousand boons' – a variety indigenous to northern Hungary from time immemorial but, as I wrote earlier, originating I believe in India. This is one of those extraordinary situations that one comes across from time to time in one's viticultural studies: grown in other parts of Hungary and other countries in south-eastern Europe, *Ezerjó*, a yellow grape, produces a mediocre, characterless sort of wine, but by great good luck, one of the Bavarian settlers must have introduced it here, where it flourishes in a most remarkable way and makes a wine – Móri Ezerjó* – of excellent quality, dry and of fine bouquet and flavour. The aspect of the Mór vineyards is good, too, as they were established on the steep south-facing slopes of the Vertés hills, where they are sheltered from the north, and they are fairly high, 200-250 m above sea level. In very good years it will produce some sweet 'aszu' wine, but I like it best when it it dry.

Eger

This is a beautiful baroque town up in the northern massif and

*-i after a place name is the Magyar possessive suffix like the German -er. Thus 'Móri Ezerjó' means 'an Ezerjó wine from Mór'.

famous as the home of Bull's Blood – Egri Bikavér – but the Eger wine district comprises twelve surrounding hill villages and has 3150 hectares of vineyards. There are records of winemaking here before the Magyar conquest and that it was started by 'Franks who settled there after seceding from the episcopate of Liege' – probably the same Walloons who brought Furmint to Tokaj; Eger is not far from Tokaj. The soil here is of soft volcanic rock – trachyte and rhyolite – excellent red wine soil and easily carved to make the extensive underground cellars which are one of the features of Eger.

As well as the dark red wine for which it is famous, the district grows other red and 'Siller' wine, and white wines from *Leányka* and *Mézes Fehér*, which here make rich dessert wines; *Wälschriesling* and *Ezerjó* and the Balkan *Kovidinka*. But its fame rests on its red wines, and so I shall look at them in some detail. The principal vine is *Kadarka* and it has grown here for centuries and makes excellent aromatic Siller wines for consumption soon after it is made, and full-flavoured red wines which benefit greatly from maturing in cask and bottle for a few years.

Three of the noble French *cépages* are grown in the Eger district, principally *Pinot Noir* (*Nágyburgundi*) with the Bordeaux *Merlot* (*Médoc Noir*) and *Cabernet*. Bikavér (Bull's Blood – although I am told this is a pretty 'free' translation) is made by pressing together grapes from *Kadarka* (70%), *Pinot Noir* (15/20%) and *Merlot* (10/15%) producing a wine of high extract, moderate acidity but no higher in alcohol than most Hungarian wines, about 12.5° to 13° G.L. I have no doubt at all that this would keep well for years and mature beautifully in bottle. It is one of the stupidities of the present attitude to wines that do not come from France that they are generally assumed to be ready to drink when they are young. If the best of Hungarian red wine (and indeed of some from other central European countries) were given even some of the care that is as a matter of course lavished on the least of Bordeaux *petits châteaux* and the humblest of Côte d'Or *commune* wines, British wine drinkers would have fine mature red wines to drink at very low cost. Let some of the real wine merchants, who are so successfully surviving the bull-dozing attacks on the retail trade of the big groups, ponder this fact and take steps accordingly.

HUNGARY

They will have some pleasant surprises and their customers will bless them. But to return to 'Bull's Blood'. The Hungarians know the value of keeping this wine and they claim that it acquires with age a 'fragrance not unlike cloves or vanilla'. Well, I have seen worse descriptions of the aroma of a mature Claret. The legend of Egri Bikavér dates from 1552, when the fortress of Eger, defended by the Hungarian hero István Dobó, was besieged by 'overwhelming' forces of the Turkish Army under Ali pasha. It is said that the men, encouraged by quantities of Egri Bikavér continuously served to them by their women, who even in the later stages of the siege fought alongside them, withstood the Turkish onslaughts, Ali pasha withdrawing in disorder and the fortress of Eger remained unconquered.

Mátravidék or Mátraaljai

A large area, 12,300 hectares, in the northern massif, adjoining the Eger district on the foothills of the Mátra mountains, it is the biggest wine-making area in Hungary after the huge vineyards of the Great Plain. Formerly it was divided into two areas, Gyöngyös-Visonta and Debrö. I have no information about how ancient is the vine-growing and wine-making here, but without claiming origins in Roman times, it certainly has a very respectable ancestry. The soil differs from that of Eger being variously loess and gravel on subsoils of miocene marl and Pannonian sand and clay. There are some sites of vinous importance, but this area grows a lot of *Chasselas* for table grapes and also at Verpelét, I am told, tobacco of excellent quality. The best-known wine of the district is Debröi Hárslevelü, a wine of very good quality, made from the 'lime-leaved' vine that provides one of the Tokaj grapes, a variety indigenous to Hungary. It is a sweetish, aromatic wine of a green-white colour and deserves to be better known on our market. The neighbourhood of Gyöngyös makes very good wines from *Kadarka* and *Mézesfehér*, but in general, and apart from the two sites mentioned, this area produces quantities of good quality table wines from *Wälschriesling* (quite dry here) and *Leányka*. Other names in this district likely to be found on Hungarian wine labels are Visonta, Abasár, Nagyréde, Kisnána and Verpelét.

Mecsek – Villány-Siklós – Szekszárd

Three important areas to the south of Transdanubia in the angle of the Danube and the Drava and towards the Slavonian frontier; the first two were formerly known as the Pécs-Villány district and under that name their wines are well known on the British market. Most of the vineyards in these areas date back to pre-Roman times – before the famous wine-encouraging Emperor Probus who came from Pannonia of which this district formed part.

The Pécs vineyards are extensive, including those of five hill villages as well as the vineyards growing round the town of Pécs itself (Fünfkirchen in Hapsburg days), an important ancient city which still shows evidence of 150 years of Turkish occupation. They grow on the foothills of the lovely Mecsek hills on a subsoil of loess with typical Pannonian deposits, and produce white wines of high quality from *Wälschriesling, Furmint* and *White Pinot,* all of which are well-balanced wines of the style that exactly suits the British taste. They also grow here a grape called *Piros Cirfandli,* the wine of which I have not tasted.

Villány is famous as a red wine district and makes the best red wine of Hungary from *Pinot Noir* – Villányi Burgundi. As I wrote of the red wine of Eger, Villányi Burgundi is a wine which at its best has fine characteristic Pinot quality and high extract and it is absurd not to treat it as it deserves, as we treat wines from Burgundy, many of them inferior, in my opinion, to the Villány Pinot. Red wines of almost as high quality are made here from *Kadarka* and others from the Austrian *Blau Portugieser,* which I find a little coarse.

Siklós, now paired by the Hungarian authorities with Villány, makes some white wine in addition to the red wines for which this area is famous, but I am told that this district is now being increasingly made into an area of red wine production, which is a good thing. Hungary has plenty of other excellent white wine growing areas and there are few enough European vineyards outside France that can make red wine as well as it is made in this part of Hungary.

Szekszárd, the third of this group, a little to the north west of the Pécs area, is also an ancient red wine producing district, making excellent full-bodied wines from *Kadarka* which are said to have been greatly favoured by the Roman Emperors. (It is interesting and significant to learn how much the Roman Emperors depended on Hungary for their best wines. It does not surprise me.) If the red wines of Villány are of the style of Burgundy, those of Szekszárd may be said to be more in the Bordeaux style. The best known is Szekszárdi Vörös, high in extract and about 13° G.L. in alcohol; this is another wine that ought to be kept to mature. It is one of several red Hungarian wines praised by Franz (Ferenc) Liszt. There is a little white wine production here, but it is of much less importance.

Somló

This is a small district of a mere 435 hectares, but one of Hungary's most important sites, producing wine of outstanding quality, with legendary qualities second only to those of Tokaj.

It consists of an extinct volcano 435 m high topped with an ancient ruined castle, a prominent feature in the surrounding Transdanubian plain to the north of Mount Badacsony. Mount Somló appears to be of a different shape viewed from different directions. From the village of Oroszi it 'assumes the outlines of a lovely woman's breast'. The core of the hill is of basaltic rock with topsoils of decayed lava, loess and Pannonian sand. Its slopes are covered by vineyards and the principal village is Somlóvásárhely, which with three other hill villages, Szölös, Doba and Oroszi, forms the wine district. The origins of Somló wine-making are ancient; Hungary's first king St Stephen (István) is recorded as having founded a nunnery at Somlóvásárhely so that the nuns could tend and supervise the cultivation of the vineyards. It is also interesting to note that in the 13th century the vineyards came under the supervision of a French monk 'an outstanding master at wine-growing' brought there by the Abbot for that purpose. Later, in Maria Theresa's time, the Somló vineyards were owned by the Esterházy family: the area is rich in history. These vineyards have always been regarded by the Hungarians as unique. Over the centuries strict laws have been applied to protect the quality and reputation of Somló. I suppose that, next to Tokaj-Hegyalja, they produce

Hungary's finest wines: in fact it is one of those rare sites, found occasionally in the best European wine countries, where a combination of local climatic conditions and geological structure predestine it to make wine of extraordinary quality.

The best Somló wines are made from *Furmint,* and a great deal of high quality *Wälschriesling* wine is also made. Lesser quantities of *Traminer, Rhineriesling* and the oddly-named *Juhfark* (lamb's tail) are also grown, with a little *Budai Zöld, Mézesfehér* and even *Ezerjó.* The style of Somló wines varies with the aspects of the vineyards. On the south-facing side it produces big dessert wines, while on the western slopes wine of quite different, drier styles are made. All the Somló wines need time to make and mature and are therefore relatively expensive – but not by comparison with wines of similar high quality made in western European vineyards. The Emperor Franz-Joseph kept our own Queen Victoria supplied with Somló wines and she was very fond of them. There was a family tradition in the House of Hapsburg that their princes and archdukes should drink a glass of Somló wine on their wedding nights to promote the procreation of male offspring. The present down-to-earth Hungarians, although sceptical of the scientific basis of such a tradition, nevertheless record the statistic that male exceed female births in these villages 'a fact that boosts the value of that district in the eyes of mothers of daughters'. Somló wines are also famed as promoters of longevity. So anybody wishing to live to a ripe old age after raising a family of sons can hardly go wrong with it.

Sopron

An area of 1300 hectares in the extreme north-west; all that Hungary has left to her of the Burgenland. Sopron lies in the Alpine foothills to the south of the Neusiedlersee, which in Hungary is called Lake Fertö (see the chapter on Austria), and its wine-making can be traced back to the pre-Roman Celts. It has been lucky in escaping the worst of the disasters that have so troubled Hungarian history, including the Turkish occupation, and the development of vine-growing here has an almost unbroken record extending over one thousand five hundred years. The traditions of Sopron are closely bound up with those of the neighbouring Burgenland vineyards, now in

HUNGARY 81

Austria, and from her geographical position it is clear why the wines of Sopron were those that first spread the fame of Hungarian wine into Europe. The present town, very pleasant and rich in architecture of many periods, is built on the site of Roman Scarabantia and has, since the Middle Ages, been an important stopping place on the international commercial routes. Sopron has special interest for musicians, as Liszt started his amazing career at nearby Kismarton in 1819 under the patronage of the great Esterházy family, under whose enlightened patronage, to their great credit, the great Joseph Haydn worked for thirty years or so in their nearby palace at Fertöd. He is buried nearby.

The Sopron wine-makers for centuries were specially privileged and the quality of the wines was very strictly controlled. The Hungarians appear always to have been well aware of the superiority of these wines and have taken trouble to preserve their qualities. Wines of many styles have been – and still are – made in this district, but its fame rests on a red wine, Soproni Kékfrankos. This 'blue French' grape is a type of *Gamay* and makes excellent wines which clearly show their relationship to their French cousins. Unlike the other fine Hungarian red wines, Soproni Kékfrankos is a wine to be drunk young and fresh. It is well known and popular with British consumers and has over the centuries had many famous admirers, from the great astronomer Kepler in the 17th century and Napoleon Bonaparte (who thought highly enough of it to mention it in his memoirs) to Franz Liszt.

Some pleasant white wines are made here, too, from *Wälschriesling*, *Traminer* and the Austrian *Veltliner; Sylvaner, Muskat* and even *Furmint* are also grown, but the importance of Sopron lies for us in its red *Gamay* wine.

The Great Hungarian Plain

The 'Alföld' with 95,000 hectares of vineyards is one of the geological oddities of central Europe. Its topsoil is mostly of sand on strata of clay, pebbles and loess, filling a deep depression which I am assured is thousands of metres deep in places, in the surrounding mostly volcanic hills; a huge monotonous plain covering most of south-eastern Hungary, south of the northern massif and between the Danube and the Romanian border. Clearly this is problem land from the point of view of agriculture, and it is subject to its own special climate which is unpredictable with a long, rigorous winter and hot summers, sometimes parching the land with prolonged droughts.

Although a great deal of the vine growing is post-Phylloxera (you will remember I mentioned earlier that sand lands such as this are almost immune from the Phylloxera aphid), and much of the wine made from grapes grown on these vines is of no very high quality, but much drunk and enjoyed in Hungary, sometimes in the national custom as long drinks with mineral water, there are nevertheless some areas producing wine of good quality and vineyards established as long ago as the 11th century.

In my appendix on soils I will try to indicate some of the problems that occur in growing crops of any sort on a soil structure of this kind, but clearly one of them is the necessity to bind the sandy topsoil and keep it from drifting in high winds. The story of Hungary's long struggle to tame and make useful this great area of sand plain, with the many set-backs that they suffered (not the least of which being the enforced neglect during the Turkish occupation), this story is, as they themselves claim, an epic. One of the important discoveries was made by a Swiss immigrant in the latter part of the 19th century who successfully explored the possibilities of cultivating vines on the sand land and the study of the ways that the vine binds the sand, with its deep and wide-ranging root systems, bringing rich crops to hitherto arid, almost desert land. But while most of the wine made in this vast area will be on little interest to us, some of them may be of greater interest and they are in any case worth listing. Half of the total area of vines is planted with *Kadarka,* and this is mostly in the southern part of the Plain between the Danube and the Tisza rivers from Keskemét as far southwards as Szeged, another good area almost on the Slavonian border; in fact Keskemét is one of the very ancient vine sites – a sort of oasis – with vines and other fruit cultivated there for hundreds of years. Naturally with such growing conditions wines of high extract are not made, but in good vintages both full-bodied and Siller *Kadarka* wines of some quality are produced. Excellent dessert grapes are grown here, many from

HUNGARY 83

local hybrids mostly by *Chasselas* and *Muskat* crossings. For white wines, *Wälschriesling* is very widely grown, and some local varieties – *Leányka, Muskat-Ottonel, Mézesfehér* and *Ezerjó,* and the lesser *Kövidinka, Sárfeher* and *Szlankamenka.* A Riesling of high quality is made at Jászberényi to the north of the Alföld, where there are ancient traditions of wine-making, and another at Csengöd farther south. The wines of the Alföld are usually of lower alcoholic strength than the general run of Hungarian wines, sometimes as low as 10% G.L. and of course except in exceptional cases, low in extract.

The Hungarians have a sparkling wine-making tradition (and they still quite shamelessly call it 'champagne') which they claim was founded early in the 18th century at the State Wine Cellars at Budafok, near Budapest and near the town of Pécs in Transdanubia. A great deal of sparkling wine is still made in these places by the original champagne method but they have more recently established modern 'Charmat' closed tank equipment. Hungarian sparkling wines have a high local reputation but are most unlikely ever to find a place on the British market.

These notes about the Hungarian wine districts are based on up-to-date information given to me by the Hungarian authorities. The anecdotes, however, come from the interesting *Hungarian Wines through the Ages* by Zoltán Halász, and quotations in the text between single commas are from that often very amusing work.

7
HUNGARY
TOKAJ-HEGYALJA

HAVING read everything I can find that the Hungarians – and others – have written about Tokay (which I will call it instead of the pendantic Tokaji) and experienced the poetical extravagances that even thoughts of it appear to have the power to instil into their writing, I shall try to set out dispassionately the facts of the geological and geographical background and the techniques that go into the making of this extraordinary wine, and then perhaps let myself go a bit in relating its history and a few of the many legends associated with it.

The Tokaj-Hegyalja wine district has an area of 6,225 hectares and a production in 1969 of nearly 200,000 hectolitres.

The name covers all the wine produced in twenty-eight hill villages. The first part of it is taken from one of them – Tokaj – which strangely enough is said not to produce the very finest wine, but it was a fortunate choice for it makes a word that everybody can pronounce and remember. The other part of the name – Hegyalja – is the Magyar word for 'foothill district' and it is on the southern foothills of the Eperjes-Tokaj range of volcanic hills, protected to the north by the high Carpathians, that the vineyards are planted. These hills extend in Hungary for nearly 20 km in a north-easterly direction from Szerences up to the Czechoslovakian frontier and beyond. A little Tokay-style wine is said to be made in Slovakia, but of course it is not Tokay! Thus the vine-clad slopes have the ideal south-easterly aspect. The hills are not high, the highest and most southerly,

HUNGARY: TOKAJ-HEGYALJA 85

Kopaszhegy (which means Bald Mountain) 516 m and the vineyards are planted between 150 and 300 m above sea level. Flowing through this picturesque country is the Bodrog river, a tributary of the Tisza. The most important of the villages, apart from Tokaj, are Sárospatak the cultural and political centre of the district, where the first Tokay as we know it is claimed to have been made in 1650; Tállya, Tarcal, Olaszliszka, Erdöbenye, Tolcsva, Zambor and Mad which, with a place called Mezes-Malé, was the site of the Hapsburg Emperors' vineyards, I suppose where 'Imperial Tokay' was made.

The climate is basically dry with hot summers, sunny extended autumns (2,700 hours of sunshine in a year is claimed) and cold stormy winters. This climate is certainly an important factor in the formation of the qualities of Tokay. Another is, of course, the geological formation of the land, with subsoils of rhyolite and trachyte rocks and top soils of decayed lava and loess: most of Hungary's finest vineyard sites are on volcanic rocks of one sort or another.

The vine varieties grown here are strictly controlled and it is illegal for other vines – or wines for that matter – to be brought into the area. There are three only: *Furmint*, the principal one, we have encountered in many places before, but here it found its first home in central Europe, having been brought by the Walloon wine-growers invited into the district by King Béla IV after the devastation following the Tartar invasion of the 13th century. (I have hitherto assumed that these Walloons came from what is now northern France, but there is doubt about it and some authorities claim that they came from Italy: another of the many instances where further research is needed.) But there is evidence that French settlers came into the district even earlier. The second is the indigenous *Hárslevelü*, the lime-leafed vine, and the third a small quantity of *Sárgamuskotály* (a yellow Muscat) which I think is a fairly recent introduction as I find no mention of it in earlier 19th century records.

There are several kinds of Tokay wine. In descending order of excellence, there is Tokay Essence (Eszencia), then Tokay Aszú in several degrees of intensity, Tokay Szamorodni, sweet and dry, and Tokay Furmint.* The first two of these, Essence and

*I hear that the Hungarians are now separately vinifying the *Hárslevelü* and offering it as Tokay Hárslevelü. I have not yet tasted it.

Aszú, are the legendary wines of Tokay, and the making of them involves unique and quite complex techniques. I shall deal with them first.

Essential to the making of 'aszú' wines (in Hapsburg days it was called 'ausbruch' and both words mean 'syrupy') is the presence on some of the grapes of the parasitic fungus *Botrytis cinerea*, which the French call *'pourriture noble'* and the Germans *'edelfäule'*; both mean 'noble rot'. Only on certain varieties of grape and under proper, quite critical, weather conditions will this fungus perform beneficently and in some circumstances its effect can be disastrous. There are but a few isolated sites in Europe where the conditions are right for it, and that not every year: the conditions cannot be artificially created. The most famous areas apart from Tokaj-Hegyalja are Sauternes in France and parts of the Rhine and Moselle districts in Germany. The right conditions for *Botrytis cinerea* to work properly are: the fruit must be absolutely healthy; it must be over-ripe; sufficient but not too much rain in the July-August growing season when the grapes fill out, followed by a fine and warm September and October, with cold nights and misty dawns. The warm autumn days (but they must not be too hot) encourage the formation of the grey mould, and the rapid cooling at night beneficially retards its growth. The autumnal alternation of warm and cold, dry and moist, sums up the conditions but none of these factors must be excessive or the mould may be killed before it does its good work. And its good work is this. The fungus penetrates the now very thin skin of the grapes which begins to wither and wrinkle; the water in the grape juice evaporates during the warm days, and the fungus by its action reduces the natural acids and concentrates but does not reduce the grape sugar. Thus the grape produces much less juice, but what it does produce is enormously concentrated. This way of concentrating sugar in grapes (and clearly there are easier ways of doing it) gives an invaluable bonus in a subtle and characteristic taste and aroma which nothing else can give a wine. I shall not attempt to describe it nor will I quote any of the strange images others have found to evoke it: it is indescribable. This, then, is what the Hungarians call 'aszú' grapes.

At the vintage, which by an old tradition starts on the feast of SS Simon and Jude, October 28th, if the conditions have been right and aszú berries are sufficient, they are carefully picked and kept separate from the remainder of the crop. Even the main picking is gone over again on special 'selecting tables' back where the wine is being made – what the French call the *chai* and I can think of no good translation – and any aszú berries that have been missed are picked out and added to the others. The aszú berries are collected from the vines in long wooden receptacles called '*puttonyos*' holding about 30/35 litres. These are also used later in the process as measures. The juice that oozes from the grapes in the puttonyos (and this rarely exceeds a couple of litres) and on the selecting tables, without the application of any pressure other than the weight of the grapes, is collected, put into casks of about 130 litres called '*gönci*' (I will explain more about them later) where it ferments very, very slowly, indeed for years, and I doubt if the fermentation ever completely stops. Its alcoholic content will rarely exceed 5° or at the most 8° G.L. This is Tokay Essence. More about it later; I shall now turn to aszú.

These aszú berries are trodden by bare-footed workers into a 'paste' – or they were until recently. The Hungarians have developed machines to do it now, but the essential part of of the process is to knead the 'rotten' grapes without damaging the pips. This can only be done, whether by machines or bare feet, by treating quite small quantities at a time. It is said that the test of a good aszú paste is to take a handful and squeeze it, when all that remains in your hand should be the pips. The thin skins will have disappeared or one could almost say dissolved in the pulp.

While all this goes on, the remainder, which is the greater part of the vintage, is pressed in the ordinary way – but not quite. As is normal practice in making good wine nowadays, the grapes are removed from the stalks before pressing; but in making Tokay Aszú the stalks, still green and sappy, are crushed separately, added to the must and stirred in it for six hours to extract the juices from them. I have never heard of this being done elsewhere, but the Hungarians regard it as an essential part of the process of making Tokay Aszú, and they should know.

Before describing the rest of the process, let us return to the *puttonyos* and *gönci*, which have important parts, if only theoretically, to play as measures. The richness of Tokay Aszú is expressed as being of so many puttonyos. This means that a certain number of puttonyos of aszú paste were added to a gönc measure (120/140 litres) of normal must, in theory from 1 to 6, but 1, 2 and 6 are rarely used. Thus a Tokay Aszú of 5 puttonyos consists of about 130 litres of normal must to which has been added about 150 litres of aszú paste, and the resultant wine will clearly be very rich. After a few days fermentation in open vats, the must is stirred, the solids filtered out, and the clear must filled into gönci for long, slow fermentation in the cool, low cellars, hewn out of the rock centuries ago, which I will tell you about later.

There is yet another unusual feature in the making of Tokay; the small gönci in the cellars (or as they call them locally 'rock-holes') are not topped up as the maturing wine evaporates, and a type of 'flor' forms on the wine, a process similar to what happens to Sherry, and this is yet another factor contributing to the unique flavour of this remarkable wine. I will not try to describe this flavour of old Tokay but just mention that it is remarkable, sweet without being cloying, indeed with a dry finish like an old vintage Madeira, and with a beautiful quite incomparable flavour and aroma. Let me put it this way – whoever paid £220 at Christie's Auction Rooms for a half-litre of 1811 Tokay Essence probably got good value for his money.

I must add, before going on to the other Tokays, that in making Tokay Aszú nowadays about 70% is of *Furmint* which is the variety to which *Botrytis cinerea* takes most kindly, with about 25% of *Hárslevelü* which the Hungarians claim 'moderates the sharper acids and astringency of the *Furmint*', and about 5% of *yellow Muscat* for flavour.

'Szamorodni' is a Slavonic, not a Magyar word and was originally used in connection with Tokay by the Poles. It literally means 'such as it has grown' which in practical terms means that the wine has been made from grapes picked without the selection of aszú berries. Clearly, therefore, it is not likely that much of it would be made in years when the conditions have been good for the appearance of *Botrytis cinerea,* and it will never be as rich as a Tokay Aszú. Szamorodni Tokays are regarded as table rather than dessert wines and can vary between being as rich as, for example, a Sauternes and quite dry, as, say, Meursault.

HUNGARY: TOKAJ-HEGYALJA

They are made like Aszú, however, in the sense that the fermentation is in two stages, and in the case of Szamorodni the solids (marc) are filtered or pressed out of the must after only six to twelve hours, long enough as the Hungarians put it to 'wash the sugar out of the aszú berries'. Then the clean must goes into gönci, the fermentation finished and the wine matured as with Tokay Aszú.

There is nothing strange about a Polish word being used to describe this style, as the Poles have for centuries been great connoisseurs of Tokay. The Hungarians, with an unusual modesty, are fond of quoting a Latin saying *Nullum vinum, nisi Hungariæ natum, Poloniæ educatum* (roughly 'A good wine is grown in Hungary and matured in Poland'). Two little digressions while I am on the subject of Polish association with Tokay. The Poles used to mature their best and oldest Vodka – 'Starka' – by filling it into gönci that had been used to mature Tokay, and burying them in the middens of their stables. The result is said to have been astonishing, which I can well believe. The second digression concerns the ancient firm of Fukier, a branch of the great merchant banking house of Fugger, the principal wine merchants in Warsaw since the 16th century, who are said to have had in their cellars before the last war no fewer than 328 bottles of Tokay Aszú of the 1606 vintage as well as stocks of several thousand bottles of other great vintage years, 1668, 1682, 1737, 1783 and 1811 (The Year of the Comet, a magnificent year for wine everywhere). One dares not imagine what happend to this fabulous collection in the tragic years of 1939-45; but a practical point of interest is that the bottles were kept standing up and their corks changed every six years.

Finally there is the wine – Tokay Furmint. Of course, it is not Tokay in the sense of Essence, Aszú and Szamorodni, but nevertheless a wine made in that area, from the grape variety that is the very heart of these great wines, must be interesting and so it is. It is a full bodied and fairly rich table wine, again comparable with a good Sauternes in its style, but having the unmistakable *Furmint* flavour and aroma. In developing this area the Hungarians are providing for greater production of Tokay Furmint. Wines of this style have in the last few years become unfashionable in England. This is not the place to go into the whys and wherefores of it, but I am sure that the wheel of fashion will turn and good sense in taste will return.*

We will soon be involved in the legends and history of this marvellous wine, but let me first record one or two other interesting facts. The 'rock holes' cut deep into the Tokaj mountains, in which Tokay is matured to this day, were made originally by the local people so that the valuable stocks of wine could be hidden from the armies crossing and re-crossing the country over the centuries – Crusaders, Turks, Hungarians – and they were made so small that it is impossible to stand upright in them, inevitably producing the saying that 'One has to bow before Tokay wine'; but this smallness also led to the evolution of the small local gönci casks, and by one of those natural attributes that are all too readily called 'accidents' these rock holes were found to make perfect places for the maturing of Tokay wines. The casks take their name from the nearby village of Göncz, famous for fine coopers.

Like almost all the European vineyards those of Tokaj-Hegyalja were attacked and virtually destroyed by Phylloxera in 1891 'following a year of extremely rich vintage'; but the vineyards were quickly replanted with grafted vines and I suppose the legends of pre-Phylloxera Tokays are as rich as those of pre-Phylloxera clarets, and as incapable of being proved.

One other point before we go on to the history of Tokay; let me try to clear up one or two questions of nomenclature. There is no problem nowadays; the labels will say exactly what is in the bottle; but bottles of old Tokay of one sort or another crop up in auction sales in London regularly (that £220 bottle of 1811 Tokay Essence must have sent many a nobleman delving into the relics of his great-great-grandfather's vinous adventures). 'Édes' means sweet and 'Száraz' means dry; and bottles labelled 'Tokaji édes' or 'Tokaji Száraz' will be what we now call Szamorodni sweet or dry. Occasionally 'Tokaji pecsenye' will be found and it means a low strength table wine. I do not know that anything quite like it is made now. 'Ausbruch' was used generally in the Hapsburg heyday and has the same meaning as 'Aszú', but Redding, writing in 1833 distinguishes two styles below Essence: 'ausbruch' containing 61

---

* As I mentioned in the footnote on p. 85 Hárslevelü is also being separately vinified, but I do not know how important this is. I think it would be a mistake to dilute the name Tokay by making too many versions of it.

parts of 'essence' (which I assume to have been aszú paste) to 84 parts of wine, and 'máslás' as 61 parts of 'essence' to 169 parts of wine (but other authorities define 'máslás' as meaning the Tokay made by a second using of the aszú paste after the clean must has been taken off it.) Wine made by a similar process of putting new wine on the lees after racking is also described as Tokaji Forditás. Opinions differ on the precise meaning of these old terms, but both are clearly below Aszú or Ausbruch in quality, and Máslás better than Forditás.

Myths and legends associated with the Tokaj district go back into the most remote beginnings of history and I can pick out only a few of those that seem most relevant, noting in passing that the 'Hunnic Sagas' tell that the dreaded Attila's body was buried in the river bed of the Tisza, the river having first been diverted from and later returned to its natural course for that purpose, by gangs of slaves who were then slaughtered so that the place of burial would be a secret known only to those few intimately concerned with it. Nice people, indeed.

It is certain that this is Hungary's oldest viticultural land. The Magyar conquerors were joined in their migration by a tribe of Bulgars known as 'Kaliz' who had been famous as skilled wine-makers in their native Asia. They may be said to have laid excellent foundations for the whole of Hungarian viticulture. Viticulture was found to be well established here, and the Magyars put the Kaliz people to enlarge and develop the Tokaj vineyards. We have already mentioned the Tartar invasion and the bringing in of the Walloons, but it was not until the 16th century that the fame of Tokaji wines spread into the rest of Europe when wine from Tállya reached the table of Pope Pius IX and its excellence was recognised and is recorded in the Papal archives. It is claimed, however, that the magic of *Botrytis cinerea* was discovered and the first Tokay Aszú made at Sáropatak in 1650 from grapes grown in the vineyards at Mount Oremus by one Máté Laczkó Sepsi (whose name is certainly worth preserving), private secretary at the Court of the Lady Zsuzsánna Lórántffy, the widow of György Rákóczi I, Prince of Transylvania. The Tokaj vineyards were at that time part of his domain. (Rákóczi is a great name in Magyar history and familiar to all music-lovers in Berlioz' 'Rakoczi March' from his 'dramatic legend' *The Damnation of Faust*.) The story is that because of the threat of war – never far away in those days – the vintage was delayed until November and the re-discovery of the 'noble rot' was made; and I write 're-discovery' because knowledge of its qualities are evident in the writing of Mago of Carthage and even in Homer's *Odyssey*.

From then on the fame and legends of Tokay spread. Everyone knows of Louis XIV's love and probably need of it, and his description – 'The Wine of Sovereigns and the Sovereign of Wines'; no doubt to the delight of the Gascon vignerons in Sauternes: and of Peter the Great and Catherine of Russia keeping companies of Cossacks at Tokaj to escort the transport of their purchases of Tokay from Sáropatak to St Petersburg. I am sure that the Hapsburg Emperors found the possession of such a magical property a useful tool in their endless international intrigues. There are many other stories about Tokay, and readers interested should read the relevant chapters in Zoltán Halász's *Hungarian Wine through the Ages*. I will confine myself to two only, which strike me as giving proof of the almost incredible reputation that Tokay has enjoyed; and the second of them may offer some justification of it.

It was believed for centuries – indeed up to the beginning of the 19th century – that there must be special properties in the very soil of the Tokaj vineyards, as indeed there are, but the list of diseases that it was claimed could be cured by the use of it medicinally, from gout to bubonic plague, would be interesting to list were it not so repulsive. So great and widespread was this faith in its powers that a most profitable trade all over Europe was carried on in Tokaj earth. In 1732 the inevitable German scholar, in this case one Daniel Fischer, published a 'learned' paper on it – *De terra medicinalis Tokayensis*. Up to the 17th century it was even widely believed that there was gold in the Tokaj hills which found its way into the wine, and the famous alchemist Paracelsus went to endless trouble but failed to extract it. He published a report, however, which was so obscurely expressed that it kept the myth alive for centuries.

Finally to my second story, which brings us home and to the old London firm of wine merchants, Berry Bros of St James's. Over 100 years or so they must have shipped reasonable quantities of Tokay Essence as well as Ausbruch or Aszú, and

HUNGARY: TOKAJ-HEGYALJA

many of the bottles that have come to light in recent years, possibly nearly all of them, have been of their shipping. As well as being excellent wine merchants, the partners were men of letters and I think I cannot do better than to quote from them.

Charles Walter Berry, in *Viniana* published in 1929, gives the menu of a Champagne Dinner which ends with Tokay Essence of 1811 and 1834. What a dinner! Over the drinking of it he tells of a number of miraculous cures of which I quote but one:

> A medical man, and a friend, who had sneered at the suggestion to try this wine in a case of extreme illness, actually put a little in a man's mouth, a patient who was none other than his father-in-law, when he really had come to the conclusion that he had passed away. My friend told me afterwards that the effect was like an electric shock – the old gentleman is alive today and, believe me, this is no fairy tale.

H. Warner Allen, an old friend of the firm, in *A Contemplation of Wine* published in 1951 writes:

> My aunt, aged ninety, was dying of bronchitis, and the doctors pronounced her case desperate. They allowed her to have Tokay Essence of 1811 administered in teaspoonfuls and for two days she had nothing else. On the third morning, she was clamouring for breakfast, was out of danger, and lived to miss her centenary by six weeks.

Tokay Essence has not been made 'commercially' for very many years. I wonder what happens to it now? A solemn thought!

8

CZECHOSLOVAKIA

A Socialist Republic
Area: *129,000 square kilometres.* Population: *14,300,000*

THE state of Czechoslovakia was founded in 1918 from the old kingdom of Bohemia, with Moravia and Slovakia, on the breaking up of the Austro-Hungarian Empire. The facts of her occupation by Nazi Germany before the Second World War, the seizure of power by the Communist Party in 1948 and her recent history are familiar to everybody and I need not go into her so often unhappy modern history in greater detail.

Czechoslovakia may be regarded in some ways as a link between western and eastern Europe, for she extends for over 800 kilometres from west to east and her frontiers run with those of West and East Germany, Polish Galicia, the Soviet Union, Hungary and Austria. The whole of her long northern and western frontiers are through mountainous country, broken only by the Elbe and Oder valleys, and all her viticulture is in these and the Danube Valley.

Although some of her viticulture has roots going back a thousand years, it has in the course of her turbulent history suffered many setbacks and devastations, disastrous even by the standards of central Europe and the Balkans, and it cannot really be said to have been put on a stable basis until after the establishment of the state in 1918. Czechoslovakia has an annual production of about one million hectolitres, which is not enough to meet her own needs, and she is therefore an importer of wine.

She exports virtually none to the United Kingdom and there are no indications at present that she has any plans to go for this market, but she makes good wine and would not be the first European wine-making country to export the best of her production and bring in cheap wine from elsewhere to look after her own needs. It is worth looking very briefly at her wine production.

There are four clearly defined areas and traditions. Around the town of Melnik on the valley of the River Elbe, north of Prague in Bohemia, and here the traditions are German; an area in Moravia between Brno (the Moravian capital) and the border with Austria, where the traditions are Austrian; extensive regions in Slovakia in the Tatra foothills, east of Bratislava (the Slovakian capital) along the Danube valley and the frontier with Hungary, where obviously the traditions are Hungarian; and finally the little piece of the Tokaj-Hegyalja area that history has now put within Slovakia.

I have been given no geological details, but clearly the vineyards of Moravia and western Slovakia grow in the characteristic loess of the Danube valley, and of course the Czechoslovakian 'Tokay' in the volcanic soils of the region. It is likely, too, that the Elbe valley soil in Bohemia will be a loess.

In the Bohemian Melnik area they make good white wines from *Rhineriesling, Traminer* and *Sylvaner,* in the style of the Rheingau and Palatinate, and the climate here is similar to that of the German Rhineland – perhaps a little warmer; but they also make red wines from the *Blau Burgunder (Pinot), Portugieser* and *St Laurent.* I have not tasted them but I believe they are of good quality and very well made.

The Moravian wines are all white and made from the Austrian *Grüner Veltliner, Wälsch* and *Rhine Riesling, Sylvaner, Traminer* and *Ruländer (Pinot Gris).* They clearly resemble the Austrian Weinviertel wines of which they would, but for the incidence of national frontiers, be a part.

The Slovakian wines again are mostly white and the main production is concentrated around the towns of Modra and

Pezinok, north of Bratislava.* Here and in the more easterly districts around Bina and Sahy they grow *Wälschriesling, Sylvaner, Veltliner* and a *Muscat,* probably *Ottonel.* This is Czechoslovakia's biggest wine-making area and I am told that the wines are good, well made and typical of the wines of that part of central Europe.

Finally, in the most easterly 'Tokay' district, they grow the typical Tokay vines, *Furmint,* the Hungarian *Hárslevelü* and a *Muscat.* I do not know if in this little splinter area the growers keep up the great Tokay traditions. I hope they do. It is a perfect example of the way the vagaries of history can divide a wonderful natural phenomenom that ought to be indivisible.

*In Hapsburg days Bratislava was called Pressburg, and the Hungarians called it Pozsony when it was their capital while the Turks occupied Buda. The Magyar Parliament met there up to 1848.

9
ROMANIA

A Socialist Republic
Area: *238,000 square kilometres. Population: 19,000,000*

WHEN I was at school it was called 'Roumania': nowadays you may use whichever vowel you like. I have settled for 'Romania' because that is what they call it themselves and it seems right for a country speaking a Romance language.

There have been Romanian peoples for centuries, but the state of that name was not established until 1878 and became a kingdom in 1882. It consisted at that time of the 'Danube Principalities' of Wallachia and Moldavia, with part of Dobrudja, south of the Danube delta. As a result of two world wars and the power of Russia, she has gained and lost much peripheral territory, which we need not detail here, but she is left now with most of Transylvania and the Banat on her western, Hungarian and Slavonian, frontiers, together with the original Principalities and a little bit of Dobrudja on her Bulgarian frontier.

Romania has a long frontier with the Soviet Union on the north and east, where the boundary is the river Prutal and her south-eastern limit is the Black Sea. Most of her frontier with Bulgaria and all of it with Yugoslavia is the great river Danube. She is very proud to recognise her origins in the Roman provinces of Dacia and Scythia Pontica.

As I wrote earlier, her people speak a Romance (Latin)

language, spiced with Slavonic, Turkish, Magyar and French. They are mostly Orthodox Christians. She was from the 15th century until near the end of the 19th under Turkish occupation and, latterly, 'benevolent suzerainty': her misfortune is to be so placed geographically as to be that most uncomfortable entity, a buffer state.

However, she has compensations. She is almost as large as the Yugoslavian Federation and much more compact, and being rich in natural resources, including petroleum and other valuable minerals, has less need than some of her neighbours to rely on her agriculture. However, the soils of Wallachia and Moldavia have been described as among the richest in Europe, and Transylvania contains fine corn-growing land. But good wheatlands are unlikely to make good vineyards, which is what we are interested in. Nevertheless, the Romanians have very ancient wine-making traditions, which they claim to trace back to the third millenium before Christ, which would put them among the earliest known wine-makers. This is certainly a most ambitious claim but it is of more interest to prehistorians than to us. There is no doubt, however, of substantial evidence of wine-making in Dacia before the Roman conquest in 101 A.D., with continuing traditions extending up to today. Romania is sure of her place among the first European wine-makers.

Geographically, Romania is divided by the Carpathians and the Transylvanian Alps, with the Moldavian and Wallachian plains to the east and south up to the Danube valley; the plain of the Banat to the south-west; and a long stretch of plain and foothills up to her frontier with Hungary; with many river valleys and plateaux. To the west she enjoys the Pannonian climate and to the east the more extreme Mediterranean conditions.

From the evidence I have it seems clear that in Romania the 'socialisation' of vine-growing (as compared with wine-making and marketing) has been taken farther than in Hungary and most of the Yugoslavian States. State farms, cooperatives and 'wineries' (a horrible word, but I do not know a better) are large, well organised and equipped. There is, in conjunction with this, a system of education in the arts of vine-growing and wine-making from the most elementary up to the highest standards. While they are at present consolidating and replanting many vineyards, I do not believe the Romanians have plans greatly to extend them. They mean to ensure that those they have are well and economically managed, and produce good wine suitable for the various demands of the world markets. Romania grows grapes for the table as well as for wine-making. Clearly with State management to this extent, control of quality is much easier than it is in countries with less direct involvement by the bureaucracy. I do not claim that this is a good thing: I merely state facts.

At present about 300,000 hectares of land is planted with vines, but producing table grapes as well as about 6 million hectolitres of wine (dividing the production by the area is therefore of no value to us statistically). Of this wine production 1,500,000 hl. is of high quality; 1 million hl. for distillation, making vermouth etc. and the rest, more than half, ordinary wines for home consumption. She is a wine-drinking country to about the extent that Austria is, and she exported 2,800 hl. to Great Britain in 1970.

The Vines

There are several interesting indigenous varieties, and Romania is far enough to the east to be able to claim with some justice that she can prove their descent from basic oriental varieties. As most of her scholarly books are available, indeed many of them originally written, in French, there is not the language problem of some of the other countries studied. This kind of detailed research is really outside the scope of this book, but one example is instructive and may be interesting. The Romanians have a group of 'noble' vines closely related and called variously *Coarnă, Som* or *Grasă*, depending on where they grow, and with similar characteristics to, and producing wine like, the Hungarian *Furmint*: in fact by all normal criteria they are *Furmint*. They claim that all of them have evolved over the centuries from the oriental *Grasă*, introduced into Transylvania in prehistoric times. Yet the Hungarians claim that *Furmint* was introduced from western Europe by Walloons in the 13th century. Did they all evolve separately and far apart? Nobody can ever know, and I only mention this as an example of the danger of asserting categorically that such and such a vine is native' to such and such a place. There have been enormous movements of *V. vinifera* varieties all over Europe. I shall refer to all these vines as *Furmint*.

Other widely grown local vines are *Fetească*, two white sub-varieties *albă* and *regală*; *Fetească neagra* making red wine.* A similar vine in Hungary is called *Leányka*. *Tămîioasă Romaneasca* (there are other sub-varieties) and *Frîncușă* are two other vines claimed, with *Fetească*, to make high quality white wines.

Other native vines make ordinary locally-consumed table wines and I will not burden my readers with their names. Among native vines making red wines are the *Fetească neagra, Barbeasca neagra* and *Negru Virtos*, but the last two are largely being replaced by the better-known and more acceptable French *cépages*.

Of the vines generally grown in the central and south-eastern European vineyards, the most important are *Muskat Ottonel*, which makes particularly good wine in Romania; *Furmint* which I have commented on above; *Kadarka*, grown mainly in the Banat where the Hungarian influence and tradition are strong; and the Austrian *Neuberger* in Transylvania.

But, apart from the native *Fetească* vines, most of the new planting and replanting is in the better-known European vines: for white wines inevitably *Wälschriesling* and a little *Rhineriesling, Pinot Gris* (sometimes called by its Austrian name of *Ruländer*), *Sauvignon* and *Chardonnay* in the extreme south-east, where it is said to do well, as it has been found to also in neighbouring Bulgaria. *Sylvaner* and *Traminer* are planted in Transylvania but I do not know how extensively nor how successful they are.

For red wines, *Cabernet Franc* and *Cabernet Sauvignon* are extensively grown, and some *Merlot. Pinot Noir* but not, as far as I can discover, *Gamay*. The climate and soils of Romania, or at any rate the more western part of it, are of the kind to produce red wines suitable for our market rather than the kind of light, acidic white wines that we need.

The vine-growing parts of Romania are widely spread over the country and they produce wines of widely differing qualities and styles. I will deal with them from west to east, from the temperate Pannonian to the fiercer Mediterranean climates.

* In Romania and Bulgaria wines are either white or black (not red)!

Roughly one-third of Romanian vineyards are on mountain sides with high rainfall and low (6° C. or under) average temperatures; rather more than a third on tablelands with more normal rainfalls and somewhat higher average temperatures (7° – 10° C.); and the rest on the plains with normal rainfalls and average temperatures around 10° – 11° C.

The Arad Area

This lies around the town of that name in the north of the Banat, and the vineyards are on slopes of the foothills of the southern-most spur of the Carpathians. The soils are described as 'poor, heavy and shallow on eruptive rocks' which, I would have thought, in that climate could produce good red wine. I have not tasted them and as far as I can discover this is not one of the areas that the Romanians are making any great efforts to develop. They grow *Kadarka* and *Cabernet Sauvignon*.

South Oltenia

This is the south-western plain, starting where the great Danube gushes from the restricting mountains at Turnu Severin (the 'Iron Gate'), slows and spreads into the fertile Romanian plain; fed by many rivers, great and small, rising in the Transylvanian Alps, the biggest the Olt from which this area takes its name. It was always a peaceful part of Dacia with its natural isolation by mountains and river, heavily colonised by the Romans and with ancient wine-making traditions. It was reputed to make the best red wines of the whole country, until it was devastated by Phylloxera in 1884. Since then and until recent years it was neglected and not replanted with Phylloxera-resistant stock. It appears to be good wine-land – and not good for much else – so that Romanians may well be wise in their policy of bringing it back to life again. Part of it is sand land, but as Phylloxera cannot survive in it, this cannot have been an important part of the area. Place-names to note are Oravitza, Drincea, Rogova, Sadova and Segarcea, which will locate it on the map. A pleasant rosé from Sadova and a *Cabernet* from Segarcea are available in Britain.

Drăgăsani and Argeș

The Drăgăsani vineyards grow on foothills and terraces along the west bank of the Olt river and many of them are old established. This is one of the areas where the Romanians are extending and improving and they have experimental vineyards and a viticultural technical school there. They make traditionally red and white wines from their indigenous vines for home consumption, and good quality white wines for their export markets from *Muskat Ottonel* (this is excellent), *Sauvignon* and their native *Tămîioasă*, which makes an aromatic wine of Traminer style; lighter white wines from *Wälschriesling* and *Pinot Gris;* and red wines from the native *Negru Virtos, Cabernet Franc* and *Pinot Noir*. I have no information about their methods of vinification and have never seen anything like 'Siller' wines although they ship to Great Britain a rosé of no great distinction.

The Argeș vineyards are compartively new, much of the area being on land cleared as recently as 1958, terraced and planted with vines for table grapes as well as for wine-making. They are on hills on the banks of the Argeș river, a little of the northeast of the Drăgăsani area and grow for wine-making the most widely planted native variety, *Fetească regală,* with *Tămîioasă* and *Sauvignon* (which makes a strongly flavoured wine, apparently confirming the presence of Muscat in its ancestry) and *Wälschriesling*. Entirely a white wine area. I have no information about the types of soil.

Transylvania

On tablelands and river valleys between the Carpathians and Transylvanian Alps and on roughly the same latitude as the good winelands of Hungary and Slovenia, and enjoying the Pannonian climate, around the town of Alba-Iulia and the banks of the Tîrnave rivers: this is, from our point of view, perhaps the most important wine-producing area in Romania. And this is because it produces well the sort of white wines that we like.*
There is no significant red wine production. There are four main areas, Tîrnave, Blaj and Cimpia Libertatii on sand-stone, and

---

* It is interesting to note that there is a large old-established German settlement in this part of Romania.

Alba-Iulia on red ironstone and clay. The historical viticultural fame of Alba-Iulia and Tirnave (and incidentally of the Cotnari vineyards farther east which we will deal with later) is founded on Tokaji-like wines made from types of *Furmint* (I mentioned these at the beginning of this chapter); and as this territory has in the past been part of Hungary, no doubt similiar techniques were used in making the wines. Wines of this type are still made in Cotnari and other areas in the Mediterranean climate of the south-east, but not, to my knowledge, in Transylvania. However, they do make excellent white wines which are exported to all parts of Europe and even as far afield as Japan. The Soviet Union is a big market for the excellent Romanian sweet white wines. Of course they grow *Wälschriesling* extensively here as well as the native *Feteasca*, both *alba* and *regala*, and *Muskat Ottonel*, and a blend of *Muscat* with *Wälschriesling* and *Feteasca* is known as 'Perla'. It is a pleasant wine, imported into the United Kingdom, and the Romanians claim that it combines 'the aroma of Muscat, the acidity of Riesling and the finesse of Fetească'. I like it and it would be interesting to know more about it than I can at present discover; for example, do they blend musts, or finished wines, or do they grow and mix grapes together before pressing? They also grow here, significantly, the Austrian *Neuberger* and *Pinot Gris* which they call by its Austrian name *Rulanda* (*Ruländer*); some *Traminer* and even *Sylvaner*, although I have not tasted it and have no knowledge of the kind of wine it makes in Transylvania.

Dealul Mare Estates

This is of the most important and expanding of the Romanian vine-growing areas, starting only about 50 km north of the capital, Bucharest, in the foothills of the Carpathians and between the towns of Ploesti and Buzău, a stretch of south-facing vineyards about 60 km long and some of them as high as 600 m above sea level, thereby mitigating some of the effects of the hot Mediterranean climate. Table grapes are grown here and, particularly on the limestone soils in the district of Pietroasa, deep, strong white wines are made from *Furmint* (*grasa*) and *Tămîioasă de Pietroasă*. Not the kind of white wines that the northern European public takes kindly to. But in the district of Valea

Călugărească (Valley of the Monks) some of the best of Romania's red wines are made from *Cabernet Sauvignon*, *Merlot* and *Pinot Noir*, grown in the iron-rich limestone of the district. The Dealul Mare area has the usual Romanian arrangement of huge modern 'wineries', an experimental station and technical college. There is also here a sparkling wine manufactory using wine made from *Wälschriesling* and *Sémillon* (which hereabouts they call *St Emilion*). I can only guess that it is sweet in the style favoured by the Russians and possibly made for the Soviet market, which is huge.

The Cotnari Vineyards

In Moldavia, well north of the other Romanian wine areas, is the comparatively small area (1500 ha.) producing Romania's greatest white wine – Grasă de Cotnari. Vineyards have been cultivated here since pre-Roman times and there is no doubt that the natural dessert wines made here enjoyed an international fame for centuries. They were, like so many of the great wines of Europe, mostly grown on lands belonging to the Church and cultivated by monks. I believe that, up to about 100 years ago, it was a dry wine, although deep in flavour and aroma. Since the vineyards were reconstituted following the Phylloxera scourge at the turn of the century, vinification methods have been changed to produce a sweeter wine, more in the style of Tokaji, which is a pity. Tokaji cannot be copied, only imitated. The wine is made from a blend of 'native' vines, traditionally 30 per cent each of *Grasă* (*Furmint*), *Fetească* and *Frîncuşă*, and 10 per cent of *Tămîioasă*. It is still carefully maintained as a purely high quality wine area.

The Odobesti Area

This is Romania's largest vine-growing area, to the south of Moldavia among the caves and foothills of the Eastern Carpathians, on loess in the valley of the river Siret. Large quantities of table grapes of good quality are produced from *Chasselas doré* in the hot Mediterranean climate, as well as much typical 'deep' white wine from local varieties for home consumption. Better quality white wines are made from *Fetească albă*, *Pinot gris* and *Furmint*; and red from the local *Babeasca* and *Fetească neagra*, and *Merlot*. I have tasted the *Babeasca neagra* wine and found it a full, acceptable sort of wine, but these 'Mediterranean' wines do not ever, in my experience, have the lightness and subtlety that we like. Important vine towns in the main Odobesti area are Jaristea, Varsatura, Virtescoiu and Cazacliu. There are adjacent areas around Panciu (noted for table grapes) Nicoresti (making sound red wines) and a little farther afield Husi (or Jusi) producing large quantities of common white wine for home consumption from local grape varieties. There are big State storage and distillation establishments in the towns of Focsani and the inland port of Galati.

The Dobrudja Vineyards

These are Romania's most easterly vineyards, situated in the hinterland of the Black Sea port of Constanta and near the Bulgarian frontier. Here ancient wine-making traditions have formed the nucleus of a big recent expansion; they already rival and may well soon exceed the Odobesti vineyards in area. The summer climate is hot and the vines are planted on limestone hills with a south-eastern aspect. While producing excellent table grapes, they make the sort of 'deep', full-flavoured white wines that are liked in these southerly climates much more than they are with us. The main town, Murfatlar, has traditionally made the sort of natural dessert wines that we have already noted in Cotnari and Alba-Iulia. Plantings in the recently established vineyards are of *Chardonnay, Pinot Gris* and *Wälschriesling* (it is interesting that *Chardonnay* grows well in this sort of situation; it is planted also in neighbouring Bulgaria). In their style, these Dobrudja white wines are good and those I have tasted have been well made: but, I repeat, they are not for us.

To sum up, I think Romania has the natural resources, particularly in Transylvania, to make the sort of white wines that are so popular in western Europe and at their best are exemplified by the *Wälschriesling* wines of Hungary, Austria and Slovenia. But her wine traditions are founded in the deeper, sweeter wines she makes so well for her own consumption and for export to her eastern customers. I think her usefulness to us is more likely to be in the supply of sound red wines. It will be particularly interesting to see how her South Oltenian vineyards develop.

10
BULGARIA

A Socialist Republic
Area: *112,000 square kilometres.* Population: *8,250,000*

SURELY nowhere is the remarkable capacity of the Balkan peoples to keep their ethnic identities through centuries of wars, revolutions, occupations and oppressions exemplified better than in the history of the Bulgarians. Twice before the Turkish conquest at the end of the 14th century, the Bulgars had ruled, somewhat precariously it is true, over most of the Balkan Peninsular north of Greece. In fact, it was in the feuds of the Balkan peoples that the Ottoman Turks found their best ally and were able to keep Bulgaria as part of their Empire for nearly five centuries. And it is as well to remember that, right through the 19th century and up to the First World War, the Turkish occupation of the Balkans had the tacit approval of the Western Powers as a bulwark against Russian expansion. The modern state of Bulgaria, like that of Romania, was not really created until 1878 and was then likewise under the suzerainty of the Sultan; and the history of Bulgaria since then roughly parallels that of her neighbour (and I do not forget that in the First World War they backed different horses). There were territorial disputes with Yugoslavia and Romania, and the present shape of the country was only agreed as recently as 1947. The Bulgarians are mainly Orthodox Christians and their language is Slavonic.

Bulgaria's northern frontier is with Romania and consists

mostly of the Danube and the present partition of Dobrudja; to the east she has about 150 km of coastline on the Black Sea, frontiers to the south with Turkey and Greece, and to the west with Serbia and Macedonia. Her natural boundaries to the west and with Greece in the south are mountain ranges, the Balkan Mountains to the north and west and the Rhodope Mountains to the south. She has the plains of the Danube and Meritza valleys and in fact is geographically well endowed for the agriculture and particularly viticulture which are important parts of her economy.

I have no reliable up-to-date annual figures of her wine production, but it is probably something between three and four million hectolitres, and in addition to this she grows quantities of table grapes. She has a lively export trade, with the Soviet Union taking perhaps as much as half of her total export which itself is probably 70 per cent of her whole production. West Germany is by far the biggest of her European customers after Russia, and she exports to most of the countries of western Europe. She shipped 1,500 hl. to Great Britain in 1970, but this figure shows a slowly increasing tendency.

Bulgaria has no tradition of fine wine-making but wine has been made there since classical times. In fact as I wrote at the beginning of this book, part of ancient Thrace is now in Bulgaria and Thrace is thought to have been where commercial wine-making started; and this did not stop entirely during the Turkish occupation. The more I read about them, the more tolerant I find the Turks to have been in many ways, and particularly in the latter part of the occupation when, as I said before, they remained as the lesser of what were regarded as two evils—it was either the Turks or the Russians.

The Bulgarians themselves consume annually 22 litres of wine a head, a moderate enough quantity but I assume in addition they drink the plum brandy which in some form or another is the favourite distillate of many of the central European and Balkan countries, and I believe they are great beer drinkers.

Large-scale commercial wine production on Communist lines started in 1943, at which time there were about 450,000 peasant growers, with a long tradition of cooperatives, a sensible system for small growers all over Europe for many crops (and in Great Britain for that matter), and forming a useful basis for the

State reorganisation. Most of Bulgarian wine production is now 'collectivised' into large vineyard areas with vinification and storage installations, some of them of enormous capacity, in all parts of the country. There are more than twenty wine-growing areas of importance, but as Bulgarian wines are almost entirely sold under grape-names without indication of place of production – indeed most of them will be blends drawn from several vineyard areas – I shall not list them as I have done with the other countries. But there are some interesting 'native' vines and before going farther into details of her production, I shall look at the grapes – the essential raw material.

The vines

The most widely grown white wine grape is *Dimiat*, which is the same as the Serbian *Smederevka*. It produces the wine from which the good Bulgarian brandy (konyak) is made, which may give a clue to its character. A dull, dry, sort of wine but apparently the Germans like it as it is exported to them labelled 'Klosterkeller', and it blends with *Misket* and *Wälschriesling* to produce a pleasant light white wine sold in Bulgaria as 'Euxinograd'. *Dimiat* is also grown as a table grape. The native white wine most extensively grown after *Dimiat* is *Misket* which is a red grape clearly one of the big Muscat family, for it makes wine of the unmistakable Muscat flavour and aroma. The only other local vine is *Tamianka* which I have not tasted or identified, although it may well be the Romanian *Tamiioasa;* but this is purely a guess. It is used in Bulgaria to make a rich, fortified wine popular in East Germany.

The most widely grown Bulgarian red wine grape is *Gamza*. This may be a kind of *Kadarka* as one of the synonyms of that grape is *Gomza,* according to the excellent ampelographical atlas published in Zagreb. But the Bulgarians also grow *Kadarka* as such, and the Bulgarian *Gamza* wines that I have tasted, dry and deep but not unacceptably heavy, seem to lack the *Kadarka* characteristics, but that may be another of the many, many instances of a grape changing character in different growing conditions. A better red wine, I think, is made from their own *Mavroud* or *Mavrud* grape; big and rich ruby in colour and clearly needing time to mature, which it is rarely given, but for me it represents the best of Bulgarian red wines. In the south they grow *Pamid,* the same as the Serbian *Plovdina* and make a 'Siller' wine from it for local consumption, as I have no doubt they do also from *Gamza* and *Mavroud*. They grow a couple of Russian vines – *Rczaziteli* for white wines and *Saperavi* for red. I have not tasted them, nor does Edmund Penning-Rowsell mention that he has in his excellent and most useful *Country Life* articles, though he writes that *Saperavi* makes rich red wine 'for those who like such wines'. One assumes that they are grown to make wines for the Russian market.

Probably the most interesting vines, however, are those the Bulgarians have brought in for their enormous expansion. For white wines they grow both the Rieslings, and it is unusual that the wine they are most proud of (they label it in German 'Rosenthaler Riesling') is a blend of *Wälsch* and *Rhine Riesling*. The name of course refers to the Valley of Roses, Bulgaria being the land par excellence for roses, as I think everybody knows. *Sylvaner* and *Chardonnay* are the other two western vines, and the Hungarian *Furmint*. Edmund Penning-Rowsell speaks well of the *Chardonnay* wine from Sumen in the north-east, finding it a 'pleasant fairly light wine, but not very much like a white Burgandy'. I have not tasted it and do not know that it is imported into the U.K.

For red wines, the Bulgarians appear to have concentrated on the *Cabernets, Franc* and *Sauvignon*. I have tasted a wine made from the *Cabernet Sauvignon* and found it to be excellent, well-balanced and with more than a touch of Bordeaux quality. I have no information that they have tried either of the main Burgundian red *cépages*, (the Pinots and Gamay), which is interesting as these are grown by all their neighbours more or less successfully.

The most interesting thing about Bulgarian wine production – in fact about her whole very extensive fruit-growing and processing industry, with emphasis on export is that it is almost wholly a new creation on the foundation of a more or less primitive peasant economy. I suppose we must accept the fact, whether we like it or not, that here is an instance where the methods of Communism have been successful. The Bulgarians were wise to look to experts from western Europe, mainly Germany, to establish their wine industry and all the evidence is that they have done it thoroughly and well. They are better placed than most of their immediate neighbours to meet the needs of their main customers, Russia and Germany, and to enter into the fierce competition for the world markets in good, ordinary wines.

They have, among other things, built up and greatly extended an existing production of sparkling wine (champanski!) under the brand name 'Iskra', again mostly for the Russian market, and it is remarkable that 15 per cent of their production is actually made by the champagne method.

Grapes are grown in almost all parts of the country (except where there are high mountains), on the Danubian and Black Sea plains and in the great river valleys. But it is the exception rather than the rule in Bulgaria for the grapes to be vinified where they are grown, and so it is difficult to know where the best wine comes from. The few place-names used are mostly in the Karlovo area where they produce a pleasant *Misket* table wine and a sweeter dessert wine, also made from the red *Misket* and called Hemus. Edmund Penning-Rowsell writes of a good *Mavrud* made at Azenovgrad near Plovdiv (Bulgaria's second city) in the Meritza valley. He also writes of a local red wine from the town of Melmik in the extreme south-west, said to be so concentrated that the locals say of it that 'it can be carried in a handkerchief'.

I have tasted some of the white wines that Bulgaria has sent to the British market in bulk, particularly a *Sylvaner* which is quite remarkably fresh and acidic. There is not much doubt, in my opinion, that German expertise has been applied to the making of this wine, and that some of the grapes have been picked and pressed before they are quite ripe, thus going a long way towards mitigating the 'heaviness' of wine made from fully ripened grapes in this part of Europe. There is nothing wrong with this; it is just part of the art of wine-making, and is evidence that the Bulgarians will go a long way to 'give the customer what he wants'. This practice will never produce fine wines, of course, but can help greatly in the market for good, ordinary wines.

The Bulgarians claim to have the biggest export of bottled wine in the world! Difficult to disprove, but surprising, and I can only think that sparkling wines have been excluded, at any rate for the rest of the world. But the assertion shows the sort of drive that is now behind the wine industry in this most Balkan of countries.

11
ALBANIA

A Socialist Republic
Area: *41,000 square kilometres.* Population: *1,400,000*

I mention this little Balkan country, bounded on the north by Montenegro, on the east by Serbia and Macedonia and on the south by Greece, with a long coastline on the Adriatic and its capital at Tirana (pop. 50,000), because I know it makes some wine, but apart from having tasted and not much liked some samples sent optimistically to England a few years ago, I know little about it. However, it is said to be where the *Kadarka* vine originated, and surely that is sufficient reason for including it in this book.

It is almost entirely an agricultural country and I presume it makes wine for home consumption. The samples I tasted were crude and had not travelled well. As far as I can discover, Albania has no fine wines and no record of export trade in wine. However, I am told that she exports a good grape brandy to East Germany, inevitably and incorrigibly called 'cognac'.

12
UNION OF SOVIET SOCIALIST REPUBLICS

IT would be absurd to follow the practice of quoting the area and population of this enormous Federation as we are only concerned – and that only briefly – with that part of it which can be considered in our context as part of southeastern Europe: the Republic of Moldavia (for a time Romanian Bessarabia), the southern Ukraine bordering the Black Sea, and the Crimea peninsular. They are an important part of Russia's rapidly increasing wine production, which seems to be mainly concentrated within these areas and the Soviet Republics of Armenia, Azerbaijan and Georgia, and particularly in the land between the Black and Caspian Seas, north of the Caucasus mountains.

Of the wines that are imported into Great Britain all, with the exception of a Moldavian red wine, come from Georgia and I therefore do not feel obliged to comment on them. No doubt one day a study of Russian wines will be written and published, but the subject is largely outside the scope of this study; and what little I can record is merely a précis of odd facts gleaned from a number of publications. The Russians have not responded to my enquiries.

Moldavia, the southern Ukraine and the Crimea were, like the other Balkan Countries, conquered and occupied by the Turks and undoubtedly their vineyards consequently suffered neglect; and after the Phylloxera disaster, they are said to have been replanted with 'hybrids' which I can only assume to have been *V.vinifera* crossings with American species. However, as part of the Russian viticultural expansion these areas are being replanted with good *V. vinifera* varieties.

It appears to be generally accepted that the best of Russian wines are made in the Crimea, and the production is said not to be large, but as I have no figures I cannot judge what is the criterion of size: in the context of the Soviet Union's statistics, their 'small' may well be enormous by the standards of central and south-eastern Europe generally. I believe viticulture in the Crimea was not started until the beginning of the last century by French vignerons and managers. They are reported to make there a wide range of styles from dry red and white table wines to strong, fortified Port- and Madeira-type of wines, and the full sweet wines, red, white and rosé, which the Russians are said to enjoy so much. The big district name here is Massandra and, apart from local types (including *Saperavi* that we have already found in Bulgaria) they grow *Sémillon, Riesling, Aligoté* (rather a surprising variety to find here), *Cabernet,* a whole range of *Muscats,* and *Pinot Gris.*

In Moldavia and the southern Ukraine there is said to be a very large production, but they have had problems with 'hybrids' here and I suppose these are being replaced with European varieties, *Pinot* (I do not know which), *Aligoté, Traminer, Cabernet* and *Riesling* all being mentioned as growing in these districts.

I would have liked to have written rather more about this almost unknown wine production, but I lack authentic information and, in any case, there is probably enough to digest in this book without it; and it is not at present important to us, whatever may happen in the future.

13

GREECE

A Military Dictatorship
Area: Mainland *159,400* Islands: *38,000* square kilometres.
Population: *8,400,000*

WHAT can I write about Greece, usually assumed to be the foundation of commercial wine-making in Europe? As Allan Sichel wrote in his *Penguin Book of Wines*: 'It is as though the mother of European vineyards mocked at the seriousness with which her children follow her teaching'. As with all the other countries that this book is about, I made enquiries, through the Greek Embassy in London, of the official bodies in Athens who are concerned with these things, and who, I am assured, are seriously engaged in improving everything to do with Greek wine-making. But in spite of reminders sent at intervals over nearly two years, they have told me nothing. Fortunately there are in Greece a couple of large, efficient producers and shippers who have given me much information about their own activities; this has helped me and I am grateful to them, but naturally they cannot be as objective in their outlook as one generally finds a Government organisation to be.

As Greece is part of the complex of eastern Mediterranean wine-making countries, in many ways is quite unlike the other countries covered, I am not going into her wine making in great detail. Like the other Balkan countries, Greece was under the dead hand of Turkish occupation for nearly five centuries, which accounts for the primitive nature of much of her agriculture, but she is pre-eminently a land on which things grow easily and richly, and throughout the Turkish occupation the wine-making traditions were always maintained. It is some measure of the generally neglected state of some of her vineyards that even since the end of the last war, Greece has had the problem of Phylloxera to cope with.

The country basks in the hot, mostly dry Mediterranean climate, which suits the growing of vines. Of the 218,000 hectares of vineyards, only 170,000 grow grapes for wine-making. The rest are dried or sold as table grapes. In 1970 Greece exported only about 2,000 hectolitres to Great Britain, and in that year produced about half a million tons of wine of which something over 90,000 tons was exported all over the world. Greece makes no fine wines but plenty of good wine. If and when she puts her house in order, she will, after her fashion, be a source of ample quantities of good cheap wine, and to be fair I believe the Greeks know what has to be done and are making some effort to do it. The population drink about 50 litres a head per annum, which gives a good foundation on which to build a sound wine industry.

About a quarter of all Greek wine is made on the Peleponnese peninsular; 15% in Attica, the country around Athens; the rest in Macedonia to the north, bordering on Albania, Yugoslavian Macedonia and Bulgaria; and in the islands, the most important as wine producers being Rhodes, Samos, Santorin and Crete. I believe the soil basis of most of the mainland is limestone, with volcanic rock on some of the islands, notably Santorin.

Greece has a bewildering list of native vine varieties of which a white grape called *Savatiano*, grown in the Attica district, is said to be the best. Types of red and white *Muscat* are grown everywhere, and the *Muscat* wines made on the island of Samos, right up against the Turkish mainland, are some of the best grown and made in Greece. This was the first and is still one of the very few of the Greek place names to be protected by law. No blending is allowed and the strict control here has obviously paid, as I suppose the Samos Muscat wines are the most successful and appreciated of the Greek wines that are exported: but then, when one thinks about it, there are clearly big advantages in being an island. Vines called *Aghiorghitico* and *Phileri* are extensively grown in the Peleponnese, but I have no idea what sort of wine they make. On the island of Crete I read of vines called *Romeiko, Kotisphalo, Liatico* and *Mandilari* (which makes red wine). *Mavroudi* makes red wine in Attica and I assume may be the same *Mavrud* that grows in Bulgaria, so that it is a logical assumption that it grows in Greek Macedonia.

The one 'noble' vine variety that Greece has given to the world, however, is the one that makes Malmsey which it is believed originated in the Peleponnese. The Malmsey wines were shipped from a place called Monemvasia, which gives a clue to the origin of at least one of the vine's synonyms. There is little doubt that this is the Malmsey, probably from Crete, that finished off the unlucky Duke of Clarence, and not the now more familiar Malmsey of Madeira, although it is there that it makes the finest wine. Nowadays the Greeks make from it a strong, rich sherry-like wine called Mavrodaphne. (This is not a place but the name, so the story goes, was given to the wine in the 19th century in memory of a beautiful black-haired girl called Daphne – Mavro means black.) It varies somewhat in quality and may be made in a number of places, including several of the islands, but can be excellent with a decade or so in bottle.

About half the white and rosé wines of Greece are resinated and become Retsina if they are white or, I believe, Kokkineli* if they are rosé. This is wine that has been flavoured with pine resin. The Greeks do it nowadays because they like the flavour, but it originated in the days long before the advent of bottles and corks, when the resin formed a film on the surface of the wine and preserved it to some extent from oxidisation and the effects of harmful airborne bacteria. The Romans used bitumen similarly, but as far as I know they never really acquired a taste for it as the Greeks have for resin. To me an 'acquired taste' usually implies something unpleasant that one can, given time, learn to tolerate, and that is how Retsina appears to me: I just cannot take it. But in fairness I must state that many people, apart from Greeks who live with it, say that they like it, especially if drunk very cold with Greek food. Chacun à son goût, but I believe it may have been a considerable factor in putting people off Greek wines generally, which is rather a pity because some of them are pleasant. I am thinking particularly of the Mace-

*I have been told that this means 'Cochineal' which sounds plausible, although I cannot think why the Greeks want to dye their wines pink!

donian Naoussa, a red wine made from *Popolka* grapes and usually aged a bit; it has real quality: and the *Savatiano* white wine of Attica is pleasant and I think it a great pity that 80% of it is resinated, which must kill all the subtleties of the grape flavour. Good dry red and white wines are made on the volcanic island of Santorin, and excellent wines on the island of Crete. I believe efforts are being made there to control and protect them as has been done in Samos, and there, to my taste, the best of all Greek wines are made.

To me the climate and general ambience of Greek viticulture tends to make dry white wines of too deep a flavour to suit British palates, but she can make good red wines and the sort of full, sweetish wines that the Cypriots have in recent years developed so successfully.

I hear that in the efforts that are being made to bring her viticulture up to modern standards, a number of the well-known European vine varieties are being planted, including *Wälschriesling*. One can only hope that, in this process, worth-while old vine varieties will not be allowed to disappear for ever. This can so easily happen – and has happened with all kinds of fruit in all parts of the world.

APPENDIX 1: Soils

For some time I have been unhappy about the way this very important subject has been treated in some of the writing and teaching about wine. All too easily, neat and slick formulæ tend to propounded: such and such a vine growing in such and such a soil in such and such a climate, and – hey presto! you have such and such a wine. It is, thank Heaven, infinitely more subtle and complex. If it were not, we would be approaching the stage of growing grapes and making wine in factories under 'controlled conditions' and all the fun of it would be gone, and if the drinking of wine is not fun, what is all the fuss about?

One of the earliest English books on soil was written in 1675 by the diarist John Evelyn. He called it *'Terra'* and according to him the theorists of his day 'reckon up to no fewer than one hundred seventy nine millions one thousand and sixty different sort of Earth'. 'I shall not argue this question' writes Sir John Russell in his book *The World of the Soil*, which I thoroughly recommend, if only to give some idea of the fascinating complexity of the subject. He goes on to warn his readers about the 'dangerous pitfalls of over-simplification and of imaginative but inaccurate detail'.

The study of soil must begin with knowledge of the evolution of the earth's structure – the work of the geologist – and this is the simplest part. It continues with detailed work of chemists, biologists and micro-biologists, thousands of whom labour in laboratories and research establishments all over the world, and the longer they work the more miraculous it all becomes. This is a subject in which the Russians have made enormous strides. The soil is indeed among Nature's greatest marvels.

In writing the national chapters of this book I have included particulars of soil and subsoil that have been given to me, and now I must at any rate to some extent justify having done so, without falling into the trap of over-simplification. I think I can do this best by summarising briefly the main soil characteristics of the countries and I hope that I shall have stimulated my readers into looking more deeply into the subject. Apart from Sir John Russell's book (Collins' 'New Naturalist' Series, 1957) there are several good modern works on geology and geomorphology (e.g. Longman's *University Geographical Series*), and a useful *Dictionary of Geology* by John Challinor published in 1967 by the University of Wales, and I must assume that my readers have some knowledge of plant structure and growth.

I suppose the soil mentioned most frequently has been *loess* (a German word; the French call it *limon*). It is a wind-borne desposit which happened at the time of the Ice Age and the great winds that the glacial spread caused. First identified and given its name in the Rhine valley, *loess* is found there and in the Danube valley. Elsewhere, it is characteristic of north China and the Missisippi valley. Being composed of debris pushed out by the glacial movement, its composition will vary, but it is reckoned to be good fertile agricultural soil and is characteristically a sandy, calcareous loam of yellow-brown colour, and will contain locally various mineral components as well as very fine silty materials. *Loess* will sometimes consolidate into a rock-like structure. Naturally, its thickness will vary from place to place, and, being a deposit, it will always be on subsoils of basic rock of one sort or another.

There are extensive areas of *sand* in the Great Hungarian Plain and its extensions. *Sand* consists of grains of silica, chemically inert so that it has little value as plant food and, most important, it lacks the capacity to bind together and form a good 'tilth', which is a very complicated attribute of good soils. To make *sand* into good agricultural land, therefore, it is necessary to find means of binding it so that the wind does not blow it about. As the only practical way of doing this is to grow plants on it, first it must be made capable of sustaining plant life and

APPENDIXES 121

this means introducing organic matter, which is most easily done by turning animals on to it and gradually building up a viable soil. Clearly this is a long process, but it has been successfully done, and it has been found that, once the *sand* can be made to support vegetation, vines have specially good 'binding' qualities with their wide-spreading deep-searching roots. Of course, it is very rare to find *sand* that is pure silica and nothing else to any great depth, and there are usually strata in the *sand* of plant-feeding substances. It will be seen, therefore, that by good husbandry and over a long period, *sand* can be made into useful land. Incidentally, it is because *sand* lacks the property of coagulating that the Phylloxera aphid cannot breed in it.

In and around the Great Plain and elsewhere are a number of extinct volcanoes. The volcanic rocks are the raw materials of good vine-growing soils, either as subsoils under decayed lava and other deposits or, usually on the higher slopes, by their own surfaces decomposing under exposure to the weather. The commonest of these volcanic rocks is *basalt,* easily recognisable by its columnar form (as for example in the Giant's Causeway) and it supplies elements that help to make wine of high quality. Other volcanic rocks include the *andesite* and *rhyolite* of the Tokaj-Hegyalja district.

Then there are the many forms of *limestone* or *calcareous* rocks, or more simply chalk in some form or another. These soils in the right conditions and with suitable deposits can help to produce good wine, notably good dry white wines. But I must beware of over-simplification and have not space to go into all the ramifications of a complex subject. Let me simply refer to the opening paragraph of this appendix and ask you to note that I have not written that all *calcareous* soils will produce good dry white wine.

Occasionally various *granitic* rocks will be found and these can provide good vine-growing soils. Examples are the *gneiss* and *schist* found in Austria.

Of course, there are many more, but let me end as I began with a plea for much deeper study and understanding of the subject. What a pity it is called '*soil*' which has such unfortunate connotations. I much prefer John Evelyn's '*Terra*'.

2 : The Ottoman Turks and their drinking habits

It is all too easy to assume that the condemnation of wine drinking in the Koran as a deadly sin was strictly respected by the Turkish Moslems. In any case the interdiction was not enforced on the conquered peoples and there is no evidence that vineyards were destroyed merely so that wine could not be made. On the contrary, viticulture was regarded as necessary to the economies of the occupied countries, and therefore as a taxable source of wealth. But inevitably great tracts of vine-growing country were overrun by the fighting armies, and under the Turkish rule a general state of oriental lassitude settled on the conquered peoples so that there is little doubt that as much viticulture was ruined by neglect as by positive destruction. It is also clear that under the relaxed discipline during occupation, many Turks, from the pashas and beys down to the common soldiers, fraternised with the conquered and learned to enjoy their domestic life, including wine-drinking. The sophistry of those Turks who held that the specific condemnation of wine did not forbid the drinking of spirits is, of course, well known; and it is an interesting sidelight, worthy of further study, that the use of spirits for other than medicinal reasons started in eastern Europe long before it was common in the west.

It is also clear that there was a general decline in Mohammedan disciplines in the last century of the Turkish domination of south-eastern Europe. A British resident in Constantinople in the early years of the 19th century records seeing as many drunks there every day as he had ever seen in any city of Christendom, while at marriages and funerals there was as much drinking of wine as in other parts of Europe. The same writer also mentioned the liking of the Turks for Mead: another way, I suppose, of getting round the letter of the law, for I do not know of another instance of Mead being made in wine-making countries.

3: The Lenz Moser high-culture system of growing vines

The revolutionary features of Dr Lenz Moser's system are, first, that the rows of vine are grown 3 to $3\frac{1}{2}$ metres apart, allowing normal farm tractors and wagons to be driven between the rows, secondly, that the individual vines are grown farther apart in the rows and the main stems are trained one and one third metres high before the fruit-bearing laterals are developed. (*The illustrations show these features clearly.*) About two-thirds of all the Austrian vineyards are now grown in this way and the system is being used more and more in other parts of the world, including conservative France and Germany.

Let us examine the advantages claimed, and in many ways proved, for the Lenz Moser system. As much fruit per hectare of equal quality is produced, it is claimed, on less than half the number of vines, and with a big economy in labour, the two workers needed to cultivate a hectare of vineyard under the traditional 'low culture' system being able to cultivate 3-4 hectares on hilly sites and up to 5 hectares on level ground; and of course the high-growing grapes are easier to gather, as anybody who has helped in back-breaking vintages on low-culture vines will readily appreciate. I do not think the labour-saving can be questioned; it is by now well proved. Nor is there any question that the high-culture vines produce as much fruit per hectare as the more numerous traditionally grown vines. The doubts are about quality. The theory, strongly held by Dr Lenz Moser, is that the vine roots have more room to spread and gain access to the quality-producing elements in the subsoil, and the wider spacing gives the growing vines better aspects to sun, light and air. I am not competent to judge and experiments continue. The French have found another advantage in the high-culture of vines in some of their Bordeaux sites subject to severe damage by late frosts, the high-growing vegetation being less liable to damage than that growing close to the earth.

Dr Lenz Moser is also well known for his experiments in 'green manuring' and has done a great deal of work in the perfecting of modern *V. vinifera* varieties like Müller-Thurgau and Muscat Ottonel, also the Bouvier and Zweigelt varieties that I mentioned in the chapter on Austria and elsewhere. His is one of those great enquiring minds without which progress is never made and Lenz Moser will be remembered in viticulture as long as man grows vines and makes wine.

4: Spirits

Although this book is about wines, it may be useful to comment very briefly on the spirits produced in these countries. The basic one is a distillate made from the blue plums that grow everywhere. It is known in Hungary as Szliva, in Bulgaria as Slivovo and in Serbia as Slivovica: always strong and fiery. Other fruit brandies are made, notably the Hungarian Barack Palinka, made from apricots grown in the Késkemet area, and one from pears called Császankorte. Cherry Brandy is made in most countries, perhaps the best being from Dalmatia. The Bulgarians make a concoction of damascene rose petals called Rosa. The Greeks make Ouzo, flavoured with anis, fennel and coriander, and Mastika from a distillation of gum mastic which is found on the island of Chios (both are usually taken with water as aperitifs like the French pastis); also a very crude affair called Raki (like Arrack) made by macerating figs and other fruit in young neutral spirit; one for natives only. Most of the countries made grape brandy of varying qualities, the Bulgarians and Greeks making a particular point of it.

5 : Chromatography Douglas Lloyd, Department of Chemistry, University of St Andrews

If a bottle of black ink is spilled on to a tablecloth the result is not a uniform black spot but, instead, a series of concentric rings of different colours, each ring representing one of the dye-stuffs from which the ink is compounded. This is an example of the separation of the components of a mixture by means of *chromatography*. This technique may be used to detect the components of a mixture. Two methods which are used in practice are as follows.

Paper Chromatography Small amounts of the material under test are applied near the bottom of a piece of porous paper, such as filter paper. The bottom edge of this paper is then dipped into a suitable solvent. The solvent moves up the paper, carrying the test material with it, but the latter moves up the paper more slowly than the solvent and furthermore different components of this material move up at different rates. These components thus separate out on the paper. If they are coloured materials they may be observed directly, if not special development techniques are used to make them evident. For a particular kind of paper and a particular solvent, the ratio of the speeds at which the solvent, and any compound dissolved in it, move up the paper is characteristic for this compound, so that, not only are the components of a mixture separated, but it is frequently possible to confirm their identity by the rate at which they move.

Thin-layer Chromatography Instead of paper, plates coated with a fine powder, frequently silica or alumina, are used. A small amount of the mixture to be investigated is applied to the powder near the bottom of the plate and the bottom of the plate is then dipped into a suitable solvent. This spreads up through the powder, carrying the test sample with it. The components of the sample are separated out as they are on paper and may be observed and identified just as in the case of paper chromatography.

This works with wine because certain elements in wine made from *vitis vinifera* spread up the chromatograph paper or plate to a different height from those in wine made from hybrids, thus giving positive proof.

INDEX

The letters after place names indicate the countries: Austria (A), Yugoslavia (Y), Hungary (H), Czechoslovakia (C), Romania (R), Bulgaria (B), Albania (Z), USSR (S), Greece (G). Vine varieties etc. are in italics. Wine names that are not simply place/grape names are in capitals.

Abasár (H) 77
Aghiorghitico 116
Alba-Iulia (R) 102, 103, 105
Aleksandrovac (Y) 62
Alföld (Great Plain) (H) 59, 65, 69, 70, 77, 81-3
Aligoté 114
AMSELFELDER SPATBURGUNDER 63
Am Wagram (A) 40
Apetlon (A) 43
Arad (R) 101
Arges, river (R) 102
Armenia (S) 113
Athens (G) 115, 116
Attica (G) 116-18
Azerbaijan (S) 113

Babic 57
Badacsony, mount (H) 66, 69, 70, 72-4, 79
Baden (A) 36, 40, 41
Bad Vöslau (see Vöslau)
Bagrina 62
Bakany, hills (H) 72, 74
Balaton, lake (H) 13, 65, 66, 69, 70, 72-4
Balatonfüred-Csopak (H) 66, 72, 74
Banat (R,Y) 18, 58, 60, 97, 98, 100, 101
Banatska Peščara (Y) 60
Banatski Rizling-Kreaka 60
Barbeasca neagra 100, 104, 105
Barbera 28, 51, 55
Bársonyos (H) 75

Bársonyos-Császár (H) 67, 74, 75
Bayerische Wald (A) 38
Belgrade (Y) 12, 47, 48, 61
Beli Pinot (Pinot Blanc) 50
Belji (Y) 55
BERMET 59
Bessarabia (S) 113
Bina (C) 96
Bizeljsko (Y) 54
Blaj (R) 102
Blatina 58
Blauburgunder (Pinot Noir) 26, 38, 41, 95
Blauer Wildbacher 38, 45
Blaufrankisch (Gamay) 38, 43, 44
Blue Portuguese (Blau Portugieser) 28, 38, 40, 41, 43, 44, 51, 54, 70, 78
Bodrog, river (H) 85
Bohemia (C) 18, 38, 94, 95
Bosnia (Y) 49, 58
Bosnia-Herzegovina (Y) 18, 47, 48
Botrytis Cinerea 42, 86, 88, 91
Borgonja Crna (Gamay) 51
Bouvier (Bouviertraube) 37, 38, 53, 59, 124
*Brajdica (*see *Plavina)*
Bratislava (C) 95, 96
Brda (Y) 54
Breitenbrunn (A) 43
Brezice (Y) 54
Brno (C) 40, 95
Bucharest (R) 12, 103
Budafok (H) 83

INDEX

Budai 70, 73, 80
Budapest (H) 12, 66, 67, 70, 72, 74
Burgenland (A,H) 10, 18, 28, 37, 38, 41-4, 59, 73, 80
Burgundac Bela (Chardonnay) 50
Burgundac Crni (Pinot Noir) 51
Burgundac Sivi (Pinot Gris) 50
Buzău (R) 103

Cabernet Franc 28, 51, 55, 56, 63, 70, 76, 100-2, 109, 114
Cabernet-Sauvignon 28, 51, 70, 100, 101, 104, 109
Carinthia (A) 18, 52
Carlowitz (see Sremski Karlovci) (Y)
Caucasus, mountains (S) 113
Cazacliu (R) 105
Chardonnay 26, 50, 100, 105, 109
Chasselas 69, 77, 83, 104
Cimpia Libertatii (R) 102
Coarna (Furmint) 99
Constanta (R) 105
Cotnari (R) 103-5
Cres (Y) 56
Crete, island (G) 116, 118
Crimea (S) 12, 113, 114
Croatia (Y) 47, 48, 55, 56
Croatia-Slavonia (Y) 18
Császár (H) 75
Csengöd (H) 83
CVICEK 54

Dacia (R) 97, 98, 101
Dalmatia (Y) 14, 48, 49, 51, 56, 57
Danube, river 13, 38-40, 48, 55, 58-62, 65-7, 72, 78, 82, 94, 95, 97, 98, 107, 110
Danubian States 16, 17
Dealul Mare (R) 103, 104
Debrecen (H) 65
Debrö (H) 77
Deutschkreutzer (A) 44
Deutschlandberg (A) 45
Dimiat (Smederevka) 108
DINGAC 57
Doba (H) 79
Dobrudja (R,B) 97, 105, 107
Donauland (A) 36, 40
Donnerkirchen (A) 43
Drava, river 13, 52-5, 65, 78
Drâgâsani (R) 102
Drincea (R) 101
Dubrovnik (Y) 47, 56, 57
Dunkelsteiner, forest (A) 38
Dunántuli (H) 67
Dürnstein (A) 39

Eger (H) 27, 69, 70, 75-8

EGRI BIKAVER ('BULL'S BLOOD') 70, 76, 77
Ehrenhausen (A) 45
Eisenberg (A) 36, 44
Eisenstadt (A) 43
Elbe, river (C) 94, 95
Eperjes-Tokaj, hills (H) 84
Erdöbenye (H) 85
Erdovic (Y) 59
Erdut (Y) 55
EUXINOGRAD 108
Ezerjó 51, 59, 69, 74-6, 80, 83

Falkenstein (A) 40
Fehér Burgundi (Pinot Blanc) 69
Felföldi (H) 67
Fertö, lake (H) 42, 80
Fertöd (H) 81
Feteascâ albâ (Léanyka) 100, 103, 104; *regalâ* 100, 102, 103; *neagra* 100, 104
Fiume (see Rijeka)
Focsani (R) 105
Frankinja Crna/Modra (Gamay) 51, 54
Frîncusâ 100, 104
Friula-Venezia Giulia 52, 54
Frühroter-Veltliner 37
Fruška Gora (Y) 58, 60
Furmint 27, 37, 42, 50, 53, 57-8, 62, 69, 73-4, 76, 78, 80-1, 85, 88-9, 96, 99, 100, 103-4, 109

Galati (R) 105
Gamay (see also *Blaufrankischer, Kekfrankos* etc.) 28, 38, 43, 51, 54, 56, 59-61, 63, 70, 81, 100
Gamza 108, 109
Georgia (S) 113
Gewürztraube 62
Gewürztraminer 45
Glanz (A) 45
Gols (A) 43
Gomza 108
Göncz (H) 90
Goriška (Y) 54
Gorjanci, mountains (Y) 54
Gornja Radgona (Y) 52, 53
Grasâ (Furmint) 99, 103-4
Grašica (Wälschriesling) 50
Grašvina (Wälschriesling) 50
Graz (A) 45
Great Plain (see Alföld)
Grinzing (A) 46
Grinzinger 46
Grk 57-8
GROM 62
Grüner Veltliner 37-40, 43, 51, 59, 69, 81, 95-6

INDEX

Gumpoldskirchen (A) 36-7, 41
Gyöngyös-Visonta (H) 77
Györ (H) 65

Halnturn (A) 43
Haloze, hills (Y) 53
HALOZEN 53
Hárslevelü 69, 77, 85, 88, 96
Hartsberg (A) 45
Haugsdorf (A) 40
Hegyalja (H) 84
Heiligenstadt (A) 46
HEMUS 110
Herzegovina (Y) 49, 58
Heurigen 46
Höflein, Gross and Klein (A) 43
Husi (R) 105

Illnitz (A) 43
Illyria (Y) 44
Ilok (Y) 55
Imotsko (Y) 58
ISKRA 110
Istria (Y) 13, 28, 48-9, 51-2, 54-6
Italijanski rizling (Wälschriesling) 50

Jaristea (R) 105
Jászberény (H) 83
Jeruzalem (Y) 53
Jois (A) 43
JOVACKA RUZICA 62
Juhfark 70, 80
Jusi (see Husi)

Kadarka 27, 43, 51, 58-9, 70, 76-9, 82, 100-1, 108, 112
Kamp, river (A) 39, 40
Kapela (Y) 53
Karlovo (B) 110
Kékes, mount (H) 65
Kékfrankos (Gamay) 70, 81
Kéknyelü 70, 73
Keskemét (H) 82
Kevedinka 59
Kisalföld (Small Plain) (H) 65, 67
Kismarton (H) 18
Kisnána (H) 77
Kitzek (A) 45
Klevner (see Pinot Blanc, Weisser Burgunder)
Klöch-Öststeiermark (A) 37, 45
KLOSTERKELLER 108
Klosterneuburg (A) 40
KOKKINELI 117
Kopaszhegy, mount (H) 85
Korjice (Y) 53
Kosmet (Y) 47-51, 60, 62
Kosovo Pilje (Y) 63
Kostajevica (Y) 54

Kotisphalo 117
Kövidinka 69, 76, 83
Kras (Y) 54-5
Kratošiza 63
Krems (A) 36, 38-40
Krk (Y) 56
Kruševac (Y) 62
Kutjevo (Y) 55
Kvarner (Y) 56-7

Langenlois (A) 36, 39
Laski Riesling (Wälschriesling) 50
Leányka 69, 76-7, 83
Leibnitz (A) 45
Leitha, mountains (A) 42-3
Leithagebirge (A) 40
Leutschach (A) 45
Liatico 117
Ljubljana (Y) 48
Ljutomer-Ormoz (Y) 52-3
Loiben (A) 39
Lutzmannsberg (A) 44
Lutomer (Luttenberg) (Y) 23, 53

Macedonia (Y, G) 14, 18, 26, 47-51, 60, 63, 107, 112, 116-17
Mad (H) 85
Mali Plavac (see Plavac)
Malmsey (Malvasia) 117
Malvasia 51, 55, 56, 117
Malvazija Istarka (Malvasia) 51
Mandilari 117
Manhartsberg (A) 39
Maraština 57-8
MARASTINA-CARA-SMOKVICA 57
Maribor (Y) 10, 52-3, 55, 59
Massandra (S) 114
Mátra, hills (H) 65, 67, 77
Mátraaljai (see Mátravidék) (H)
Mátravidék (H) 67, 69, 70, 77
Mattersburg (A) 43
Matzen (A) 40
MAVRODAPHNE 117
Mavroud (Mavrud) 108-110
Mavroudi 117
Mecsek (H) 67, 69, 78
Medjugorica (Y) 55
Médoc Noir (Merlot) 28, 51, 54-6, 60, 70, 76, 100-3, 105
Melnik (C) 95
Meritza, river (B) 107, 110
Merlot (see Médoc Noir)
METLISKA CRNINA 54
Mézesfehér 70, 74, 76-7, 80, 83
Mezes-Malé (H) 85
Misket 108, 110
Miskolc (H) 66
Modra (C) 95
Mohács (H) 16

INDEX

Moldavia (R) 97-8, 104, 113-14
Mönchhof (A) 43
Monemvasia (G) 117
Montenegro (Y) 18, 47-8, 63, 112
Mór (H) 67, 69, 74-5
Morava, river (Y) 61
Moravia (C) 18, 38-9, 94-5
Mörbisch (A) 43
Morillon 45
Moslavac Bijeli (Furmint) 50
Mostar (Y) 58
Müller-Thurgau 21, 25, 37, 39, 40, 45, 50, 52-3, 124
Mura, river (A) 45, 52
Mureck (A) 45
Murfatlar (R) 105
Muscat 26, 28, 45, 53, 55-6, 62, 69, 81, 83, 96, 103, 114, 116
Muskat-Ottonel 26, 38-9, 42-3, 50, 59, 69, 83, 96, 100, 102-3, 124
Muskatteller, yellow (Sárgamuskotály) 45, 50, 69, 73, 85, 88

Nagyburgundi (Pinot Noir) 70, 76
Nagyréde (H) 77
Neckenmarkler (A) 44
Negru Virtos 100, 102
Neretva, river (Y) 58
Neszmély (H) 74
Neusiedl (A) 43
Neusiedlersee, lake (A) 13, 37, 42-4, 73, 80
Nicoresti (R) 105
Niederösterreich (A) 36, 38
Nussberg (A) 46
Nussberger 46
Nyirség (H) 67

Oder, river (C) 94
Odobesti (R) 104-5
Oggau (A) 43
Olaszliszka (H) 85
Olaszrizling (Wälschriesling) 68
Olt, river (R) 101-2
Oltenia, South (R) 101, 105
OPOLO 57
Oravitza (R) 101
Oroszi (H) 79
Osogovska, hills (Y) 63
Ottenberg (A) 45
Ottonelmuskotály (see *Muskat-Ottonel*)

Pamid (Plovdina) 109
Panciu (R) 105
Pannonia 13, 34, 42, 48, 52, 58, 72-5, 77-9, 98, 102
Peć (Y) 62
Pécs (H) 65, 78, 83

Pécs-Villány (H) 78
Peleponnese (G) 116-17
Perchtoldsdorf (A) 41, 46
PERLA 103
Pezinok (C) 96
Pfaffstätten (A) 41
Phileri 116
Phylloxera 17, 20-1, 43, 63, 73, 75, 82, 90, 101, 104, 113
Pietroasa (R) 103
Pinela 54
Pinot blanc (see also *Weisser Burgunder*) 26, 38, 50, 53, 55, 59, 69, 78; *gris* (see also *Syürkebarát, Ruländer, Tokay*) 26, 50, 54-5, 69, 73, 95, 100, 102-5, 114; *noir* (see also *Blauburgunder, Nágyburgundi*) 26, 28, 38, 51, 56, 59, 60, 63, 70, 76, 78, 95, 100, 102, 104
Piros Cirfandli 78
Plavac Beli 51, 54; *Mali* 51, 57; *Zuti* 51, 54
Plavina (Brajdica) 57
Plavka 58
Plemenka 59
Pljesevica (Y) 55
Ploesti (R) 103
Plovdina 62-3
Plovdiv (B) 110
Podendorf (A) 43
Pohorje, hills (Y) 53
Popolka 118
Porec (Y) 56
Portugalka (Blue Portuguese) 51
Portugieser Rot (Kraljevina) 51, 54
Portugizac Crni (Blue Portuguese) 51
Pošip (Furmint) 57
Pošipon (Furmint) 50
POSTUP 57
Pöttelsdorf (A) 43
Poysdorf (A) 40
Pozsony, see Bratislava (C)
Prague (C) 12, 40, 95
Prellenkirchen (A) 40
Pressburg, see Bratislava (C)
Primorsko-Kras (Y) 52, 54
Prizren (Y) 62
Prokupac črni 51, 59-63
PROSEK 58
Prutal, river (R) 97
Ptny (Y) 52

RADGONA RANINA ('TIGER MILK') 53
Radgonska Ranina (Bouviertraube) 51
Radkersburg (A) 45

INDEX

Rajnai Grašvina *(Rhineriesling)* 50
Rajnairizling *(Rhineriesling)* 69
Rajnski Rizling *(Rhineriesling)* 50
Ranina *(Bouvier)* 53
Ratsch (A) 45
Ravelsbach (A) 40
Rcazaziteli 109
Rebula 54
Rechnitz (A) 44
Refosco *(Terran Crni)* 51, 55, 56
Renski Riesling *(Rhineriesling)* 50
RETSINA 117
Retz (A) 39, 40
Rhineriesling 23-4, 37-40, 44-5, 50, 53, 55, 69, 80, 95, 100, 109
Rhodes island (G) 116
Rhodope, mountains (B) 107
Riesling 23, 53, 60, 83, 114; *Italian* 25; *synonyms* 25
Rijeka (Fiume) (Y) 56
Rizvanac Bijeli *(Müller-Thurgau)* 50
Rogova (R) 101
Romeiko 117
Rosalien, mountains (A) 43
Roschitz (A) 39
Rotgipfler 37-8, 41, 51, 54
Ruländer, Rulanda *(Pinot Gris)* 26, 38, 45, 50, 53, 95, 100, 103
Rust (A) 37, 42
RUZICA 61, 62

Sadova (R) 101
Sahy (C) 96
St Emilion *(Sémillon)* 104
St George, mount (Szentgyörgyhegy) (H) 73
St Georgen (A) 43
St Laurent 38, 41, 51, 54, 95
St Margarethen (A) 43
St Stefan o. St (A) 45
Samos, island (G) 116, 118
Santorin, island (G) 116, 118
Saperavi 109, 114
Sarajevo (Y) 48, 49
Sarfehér 70, 83
Sárgamuskotály *(Yellow Muskat)* 69
Sárospatak (H) 85
Sauvignon 26, 45, 50, 53, 55, 59, 100, 102, 104
Sava, river 13, 52-5
Savatiano 116, 118
Scheurebe 21
Schlossberg (A) 45
Schmida, river (A) 40
Schönberg (A) 39
Scythia Pontica (R) 97

Seewinkel (A) 43
Segarcea (R) 101
Sémillon 26, 50, 59, 62, 104, 114
Sentlavrenka, Sentlovrenac (? *St Laurent)* 51
Serbia (Y) 18, 47-8, 50-1, 55, 58, 60-2, 107, 109, 112
Sibenik (Y) 56-7
Sieveringer 46
Siklós (H) 78
Silvanec Zelini *(Sylvaner)* 50
Sipon *(Furmint)* 50
Siret, river (R) 104
Skadar, lake (Y) 63
Skardarka (Skutari) (Z) 27
Skopje (Y) 48
Skutari (Z) 27
Slavonia (Y) 48-51, 55, 58, 65, 97
Slavonski Brod (Y) 55
Slovenia (Y) 10, 12-13, 18, 22-3, 26, 28, 34, 44-5, 47-55, 65, 78, 102, 105
Slovakia (C) 18, 66, 84, 94-5
Smederevka 61-3
Smederevo (Y) 61
Som *(Furmint)* 99
Somló (H) 67, 69, 70, 79, 80
Somlóvásárhely (H) 79
Sopron (H) 28, 44, 67, 69, 70, 80-1
Sousal (A) 45
Spätrot *(Zierfandler)* 37, 41
Spielfeld (A) 45
Spitz (A) 39
Split (Y) 57
Sremski Karlovci (Y) 55, 59
Stainz (A) 45
Stanušina 63
Stein (A) 38
Steinfeld (A) 41
Steppensee (see Neusiedlersee)
Strass (A) 39
Styria (Steiermark) (A) 18, 37-8, 44-5, 52
Subotiča (Y) 58-60
Südsteiermark (A) 37
Sumen (B) 109
Sutztal (A) 45
Sylvaner 24-5, 50, 52-3, 59, 69, 74, 95-6, 100, 103, 109, 110
Szeged (H) 65, 82
Szekszárd (H) 67, 78-9
Szerences (H) 84
Szigleget, mount (H) 73
Szilváni *(Sylvaner)* 69
Szlankamenka 70, 83
Szölös (H) 79
Szürkebarát *(Pinot Gris)* 26, 69, 73

Tállya (H) 85

INDEX

Tamianka 108
Tămiîoasă Romaneasca 100, 102-4, 108
Tarcal (H) 85
Tatra, mountains (C) 95
Terran črni, Teran (Refosco) 51, 56
Thrace (B,G) 20, 107
Timok, river (Y) 61-2
Tirana (Z) 112
Tîrnave, rivers (R) 102-3
Tisza, river (H) 13, 59-60, 65, 67, 82, 85
Titograd (Y) 48
Tokaj-Hegyalja (H) 22, 66, 68, 72, 79, 84-93, 95
Tokaji (Tokay) 27, 42, 69-70, 72, 74, 76-7, 79, 84-93, 96, 103-4
Tokay (Pinot Gris) 26, 50, 54
Tokay Aszú 85; 87-8, 92; Ausbruch 90-2; Édes 90; Essence (Eszencia) 85-7, 92-3; Forditás 91; Máslás 91; Pecsenye 90; Szamorodni 85, 88-9; Száraz 90
Tolcsva (H) 85
Traiskirchen (A) 41
Traismauer (A) 40
Traminac (Traminer) 50
Traminer 25, 28, 38-40, 43, 45, 50, 53, 55, 59, 61, 69, 80-1, 95, 100, 103
Tramini Piros (Traminer) 69
Transdanubia (H) 65-7, 69, 72, 78-9, 83
Transylvania (R) 13, 17-18, 22, 97-8, 101-3, 105
Trieste (Y) 52, 54
Tullnerfeld (A) 40
Turnu Severin (R) 101

Ukraine (S) 12, 113

Vagava 57-8
Valea Călugăreasca (R) 104
Varsatura (R) 105
Veltliner (see *Grüner Veltliner, Frühroter Veltliner*)
VIPAVAC ('KINDERMACHER') 54
Virtescoiu (R) 105
Vitis riparia 21; *rupestris* 21; *vinifera* 19-22, 24, 100, 114, 124
VLASOTINACKA PLEMENKA 62
Vöslau (A) 41
Vramac 63

Wachau (A) 36, 38-9
Wallachia (R) 13, 97-8
Wälschriesling 23-4, 37, 42-5, 50, 52-5, 59, 61-3, 68, 73-4, 76-8, 80-1, 83, 95-6, 100, 102-5, 108-9, 118
Weiden (A) 43
Weinviertel (A) 36, 39, 46, 95
Weissenkirchen (A) 39
Weststeiermark (A) 37, 45
Widen (A) 43
Wienerwald (A) 40-1
Wolkersdorf (A) 40

Začinka 62
Zadar (Zara) (Y) 56
Zagreb (Y) 48, 54-5
Zambor (H) 85
Zametna črnina 54
Zametovka 54
Zelenac Slatki (Rotgipfler) 51, 54
Zeleni Veltlinac (Grüner Veltliner) 51
Zierfandler (Spätrot) 37
Zilavka 58, 62-3
Zistersdorf (A) 40
Zöbing (A) 39
Zöld Budai (see *Budai*)
Zöldszilváni (Sylvaner) 69
Zweigelt 38, 124